JOHN STOTT

WITH DALE AND SANDY LARSEN

A Deeper Look at the

SERMON *on the* MOUNT

TWELVE SESSIONS FOR GROUPS AND INDIVIDUALS

LIVING OUT
THE WAY OF JESUS

LifeGuide®
IN DEPTH
BIBLE STUDIES

IVP Connect

An imprint of InterVarsity Press
Downers Grove, Illinois

InterVarsity Press
P.O. Box 1400, Downers Grove, IL 60515-1426
World Wide Web: www.ivpress.com
Email: email@ivpress.com

This guide makes use of material originally published as Sermon on the Mount (LifeGuide® Bible Study) © 1987, 2000 by John Stott.

This guide also makes use of material originally published in The Message of the Sermon on the Mount © 1987 by John R. W. Stott. Originally published under the title Christian Counter-Culture.

Sidebars in part one of each session ("Investigate") are from Craig S. Keener, The IVP Bible Background Commentary: New Testament, pp. 55-66, and are used by permission of InterVarsity Press.

InterVarsity Press® is the book-publishing division of InterVarsity Christian Fellowship/USA®, a movement of students and faculty active on campus at hundreds of universities, colleges and schools of nursing in the United States of America, and a member movement of the International Fellowship of Evangelical Students. For information about local and regional activities, write Public Relations Dept., InterVarsity Christian Fellowship/USA, 6400 Schroeder Rd., P.O. Box 7895, Madison, WI 53707-7895, or visit the IVCF website at <www.intervarsity.org>.

Design: Cindy Kiple
Images: © rusm/iStockphoto

ISBN 978-0-8308-3104-3

Printed in the United States of America ∞

| P | 24 | 23 | 22 | 21 | 20 | 19 | 18 | 17 | 16 | 15 | 14 | 13 | 12 | 11 | 10 | 9 | 8 | 7 | 6 | 5 | 4 | 3 | 2 | 1 |
| Y | 34 | 33 | 32 | 31 | 30 | 29 | 28 | 27 | 26 | 25 | 24 | 23 | 22 | 21 | 20 | 19 | 18 | 17 | 16 | 15 | 14 | 13 |

CONTENTS

PREFACE

On July 27, 2011, the world lost a great man. That day, the deep, passionate faith of John Stott became sight as his life on earth ended. Renowned around the world for his preaching, his love for God's church and God's Word, and his leadership among evangelicals, John Stott was used by God in powerful ways to shape the global body of believers and the scope and history of Christianity itself.

Had he been less generous with his deep knowledge of Scripture, less humble in his teaching, less passionate about the kingdom of God and focused only on building a name for himself, his influence would have been small, and his insight would largely have died with him, available to no one after he was gone. But since nothing could be further from the truth, the sadness of his passing was couched with a deep-seated celebration of his life and his legacy that continues on—a legacy of faith, ecumenism and commitment to biblical truth.

John Stott's ministry, in essence, was one of empowerment. Indeed, in his many roles as pastor, teacher, speaker, mentor, author and evangelical leader, he had one aim: for the kingdom of God to reign in every person and place on earth. To that end, he clearly and consistently communicated the truth about God from Scripture, drew others to Jesus Christ, and equipped people to love and study God's Word as well as communicate biblical truth to others. And so his immeasurable influence—his insight, knowledge, wisdom and commitment to God's Word—lives on in those he led to faith and discipled; in the ministers he trained while he was alive and in the ongoing work of the organizations he founded to provide resources and training for pastors in Majority World countries; in the thousands upon thousands of students he spoke to at numerous Urbana Student Missions Conferences; in the Lausanne Covenant of 1974, which he helped write; in his dozens of books; and surely in countless other places that most of us will never know about where he humbly spoke and ministered and was used by God to transform people.

We at InterVarsity Press consider it a deep privilege to continue to spread John Stott's influence through his books. And we are excited to be able to offer you this new study, based on John Stott's classic commentary *The Message of the Sermon on the Mount*. You'll find in these pages John Stott's *Sermon on the Mount* LifeGuide Bible Study (part one of each session), which was originally created with the help of Jack Kuhatschek and Donald Baker, as well as readings taken directly from his exposition of the Sermon in his commentary (part three of each session as well as the introduction). Parts two and four of this guide contain brand new material written by Dale and Sandy Larsen, who have themselves been influenced by John Stott's writings through the years; those sections will help you gain an even more comprehensive understanding of the Sermon on the Mount and apply it to your life in concrete ways, as John Stott himself, a man of meekness and mercy, a peacemaker who hungered and thirsted for righteousness, clearly did.

As you participate in this study, then, you will be joining the large (and still increasing) number of those who have been influenced by the wisdom and insight of John Stott, and who have come to love Scripture more as a result of his teaching. But, even more, you'll come to know in deeper ways the Jesus he loved, that you—the salt of the earth, the light of the world—might help further the spread of God's kingdom of truth wherever you go.
The Editors

INTRODUCTION

Living Out the Way of Jesus

The Sermon on the Mount is probably the best-known part of the teaching of Jesus, though arguably it is the least understood, and certainly it is the least obeyed. It is the nearest thing to a manifesto that he ever uttered, for it is his own description of what he wanted his followers to be and to do. To my mind no two words sum up its intention better, or indicate more clearly its challenge to the modern world, than the expression "Christian counterculture." For the essential theme of the whole Bible from beginning to end is that God's historical purpose is to call out a people for himself; that this people is a "holy" people, set apart from the world to belong to him and to obey him; and that its vocation is to be true to its identity, that is, to be "holy" or "different" in all its outlook and behavior.

This is how God put it to the people of Israel soon after he had rescued them from their Egyptian slavery and made them his special people by covenant: "I am the LORD your God. You must not do as they do in Egypt, where you used to live, and you must not do as they do in the land of Canaan, where I am bringing you. Do not follow their practices. You must obey my laws and be careful to follow my decrees. I am the LORD your God" (Leviticus 18:1-4). This appeal of God to his people, it will be noted, began and ended with the statement that he was the Lord their God. It was because he was their covenant God, and because they were his special people, that they were to be different from everybody else. They were to follow his commandments and not take their lead from the standards of those around them.

Throughout the centuries which followed, the people of Israel kept forgetting their uniqueness as the people of God. Although in Balaam's words they were "a people who live apart and do not consider themselves one of the nations," yet in practice they kept becoming assimilated to the people around them: "They mingled with the nations and adopted their customs" (Numbers 23:9; Psalm 106:35). So they demanded a king to govern them "such as all the other nations," and when Samuel remonstrated with them on the ground that God was their king, they were stubborn in their insistence: "We want a king over us. Then we will be like all the other nations" (1 Samuel 8:5, 19-20). Worse even than the inauguration of the monarchy was their idolatry. "We want to be like the nations," they said to themselves, ". . . who serve wood and stone" (Ezekiel 20:32). So God kept sending his prophets to them to remind them who they were and to plead with them to follow his way. "Do not learn the ways of the nations," he said to them through Jeremiah, and through Ezekiel, "Do not defile yourselves with the idols of Egypt; I am the LORD your God" (Jeremiah 10:2; Ezekiel 20:7). But God's people would not listen to his voice, and the specific reason given why his judgment fell first upon Israel and then nearly 150 years later upon Judah was the same: "The Israelites had sinned against the LORD their God . . . and followed the practices of the nations . . . and even Judah did not keep the commands of the LORD their God. They followed the practices Israel had introduced" (2 Kings 17:7-8, 19; cf. Ezekiel 5:7; 11:12).

All this is an essential background to any understanding of the Sermon on the Mount.

The Sermon is found in Matthew's Gospel toward the beginning of Jesus' public ministry. Immediately after his baptism and temptation Jesus had begun to announce the good news that the kingdom of God, long promised in the Old Testament era, was now on the threshold. He himself had come to inaugurate it. With him, the new age had dawned, and the rule of God had broken into history. "Repent," he cried, "for the kingdom of heaven has come near" (Matthew 4:17). Indeed, "Jesus went throughout Galilee, teaching in their synagogues, proclaiming the good news of the kingdom" (Matthew 4:23). The Sermon on the Mount, then, is to be seen in this context. It portrays the repentance (*metanoia* in Greek—"the complete change of mind") and the righteousness which belong to the kingdom. That is, it describes what human life and human community look like when they come under the gracious rule of God.

And what do they look like? Different! Jesus emphasized that his true followers, the citizens of God's kingdom, were to be entirely different from others. They were not to take their cue from the people around them, but from him, and so prove to be genuine children of their heavenly Father. To me the key text of the Sermon on the Mount is Matthew 6:8: "Do not be like them." It is immediately reminiscent of God's word to Israel in Leviticus 18:3: "You must not do as they do." It is the same call to be different. And right through the Sermon on the Mount this theme is elaborated. Their character (the Beatitudes) was to be completely distinct from that admired by the world. They were to shine like lights in the prevailing darkness. Their righteousness was to exceed that of the scribes and Pharisees, both in ethical behavior and in religious devotion, while their love was to be greater and their ambition nobler than those of their pagan neighbors.

There is no single paragraph of the Sermon on the Mount where this contrast between Christian and non-Christian standards is not drawn. It is the underlying and uniting theme of the Sermon; everything else is a variation of it. Sometimes it is the Gentiles or pagan nations with which Jesus contrasts his followers. At other times he contrasts them with Jews. Thus the followers of Jesus are to be different—different from both the nominal church and the secular world, different from both the religious and the irreligious.

The Sermon on the Mount is the most complete description anywhere in the New Testament of the Christian counterculture. Here is a Christian value system, ethical standard, religious devotion, attitude to money, ambition, lifestyle and network of relationships—all of which are the total opposite of the non-Christian world. The Sermon presents life in the kingdom of God, a fully human life indeed but lived out under the divine rule.

Are its standards attainable, though? Or must we rest content with admiring them wistfully from afar? Perhaps a majority of readers and commentators, looking the reality of human perversity in the face, have declared the standards of the Sermon on the Mount to be unattainable. Its ideals are noble but unpractical, they say, attractive to imagine but impossible to fulfill.

At the other extreme are those superficial souls who glibly assert that the Sermon expresses ethical standards that are self-evidently true, common to all religions and easy to follow. "I live by the Sermon on the Mount," they say.

The truth lies in neither extreme position. For the standards of the Sermon are neither readily attainable by everyone nor totally unattainable by anyone. To put them beyond anybody's reach is to ignore the purpose of Christ's Sermon; to put them within everybody's reach is to ignore the reality of our sin. They are attainable all right, but only by those who have experienced the new birth that Jesus told Nicodemus was the indispensable condition of seeing and entering God's kingdom. For the righteousness he described in the Sermon is an inner righteousness. Although it manifests itself outwardly and visibly in words, deeds and relationships, it remains essentially a righteousness of the heart. And that means there is but one solution: A new birth is essential.

Only a belief in the necessity and the possibility of a new birth can keep us from reading the Sermon on the Mount with either foolish optimism or hopeless despair. Jesus spoke the Sermon to those who were already his disciples and thereby also the citizens of God's kingdom and children of God's family. The high standards he set are appropriate only to such. We do not, indeed could not, achieve this privileged status by attaining Christ's standards. Rather by attaining his standards, or at least approximating them, we give evidence of what, by God's free grace and gift, we already are.

HOW TO USE LIFEGUIDE® IN DEPTH

The Bible is God's Word to his people. In it and through it we find life and wisdom for life. Most importantly, the Scriptures point us to Christ, who is the culmination of God's revelation to us of who he is. The LifeGuide in Depth Bible Study series has been created for those who want to go deeply into the Bible and deeply into Christ.

Going deeply will require time and effort. But the reward will be well worth it. If your desire is a richer understanding of God's Word, if you want to grasp Scripture at a level and in dimensions you've not engaged in before, these in-depth studies are for you.

This series emphasizes

- taking passages seriously as a whole

- seeing how each passage connects to and is built on the rest of Scripture

- applying the truth of each passage to individuals and to our Christian communities

How do we do this? Each session follows a four-part format:

- **Part 1. Investigate**—Getting an overview of the passage as a whole.

- **Part 2. Connect: Scripture to Scripture**—Seeing how the passage or theme connects to other parts of the Bible.

- **Part 3. Reflect**—Pondering a key theme in the passage through a short reading.

- **Part 4. Discuss: Putting It All Together**—Tying together as a group the various themes from the first three parts and learning to apply the passage to real life.

Though groups and individuals may use LifeGuide in Depth studies in different ways and formats, the most straightforward way to use the guides is for individuals to study the first three sections on their own before each group meeting. Those first three sections are best done over several days rather than in one sitting, as individuals will typically need a total of three to four hours to work through them. Part four then offers a forty-five- to sixty-minute group discussion that guides members in putting together everything they've learned.

LifeGuide in Depth Bible Studies can be used by people of various ages, from teenagers to seniors and everyone in between. Groups can be church-related home small groups and Sunday-school classes, women's and men's Bible studies, neighborhood Bible studies, and university campus small groups. And the guides can be used on a weekly or biweekly basis, or could even form the core of a retreat weekend.

AN OVERVIEW OF THE FOUR PARTS

Part 1. Investigate (On Your Own). Inductive Bible study is at the core of LifeGuide in Depth studies. Allowing for in-depth study of one passage, an inductive approach to Scripture has three main parts: we first carefully observe what is in the text, then interpret what we are to learn from what we observe and finally apply the meaning of the passage to our own lives. This is accomplished through the use of open-ended questions that help people discover the Bible for themselves. The goal is to come to the passage with fresh eyes, not supposing we know all that it means ahead of time, but looking to see what God might have to teach us anew.

Inductive study is not meant to be mechanical; Scripture is not data that we manipulate toward a certain output. Nor does it imply that we can master Scripture. Rather we expect the Word to master us. But believing that God uses our understanding to touch our hearts and that he uses our hearts to touch our understanding, inductive study can help us draw near to God. It's a tool to guide our hearts and minds toward Christ through his Word. For more on inductive study we recommend *Transforming Bible Study* by Bob Grahmann and *The Bible Study Handbook* by Lindsay Olesberg.

Part one of each session is a revised edition of the original LifeGuide Bible study guide. LifeGuide Bible studies have been the leading series for individuals and groups studying Scripture for almost thirty years. They have given millions of people a solid grasp of the Bible. The LifeGuide in Depth Bible Study series, like the original LifeGuides, honors the context of each book of the Bible and the original message of each biblical author, and guides readers into application of God's Word. Relevant excerpts from *The IVP Bible Background Commentary: New Testament* and *The IVP Bible Background Commentary: Old Testament* have been added to these studies to offer helpful historical and cultural information about each passage. These excerpts appear as callouts in part one of each guide.

Part 2. Connect: Scripture to Scripture (On Your Own). One of the most important ways of understanding any particular passage of Scripture is to uncover how it stands in the pathway of the rest of Scripture. The historical, cultural and literary background of any passage is critical, and how biblical writers draw on previous Scripture offers a wealth of meaning to readers. The purpose of part two of each session is to draw this out.

The original writers and readers of the books of the Bible were thoroughly immersed in the Scripture written beforehand. It was the air they breathed. So when they wrote, earlier Scripture passages and themes were an inseparable part of how they thought and taught. Thus, understanding the New Testament often requires knowing the Old Testament allusions, themes or direct quotations found there. And usually it is not enough to know the one particular Old Testament verse being quoted or referenced. We need to understand the context of that verse in the chapter and book in which it is found. Neglecting this can lead readers astray in their interpretations or applications.

For example, in Mark 6:47-50, Jesus walks on the lake during a storm and is "about to pass by [the disciples]" (v. 48), who are struggling for survival in a boat. Does Jesus not see them? Doesn't he care they are in danger? Why does he intend to "pass by"? What's going on? The answer is found by going back to the Old Testament. In Exodus 33:19–34:7 and 1 Kings 19:10-11, God "passes by" Moses and Elijah to reveal himself in a clear and dramatic way. Mark uses the same phrase (which his readers would recognize) to indicate that Jesus is making a similar dramatic revelation of divine character.

In making these connections, it is usually more helpful to go backward than to go forward. That is, we should first investigate Scripture written before the passage being studied was written. For instance, in seeking to understand the Psalms, we should first go to the earlier books of the Old Testament rather than to the New Testament. The psalmists knew and perhaps had memorized large portions of Genesis, Exodus and so forth. That was the raw material they were working with; those were their sources. If we don't understand how and why they built on these, we won't understand fully what they are saying.

Take the "suffering servant" of Isaiah 52–53. Although New Testament writers linked Jesus to the suffering servant, we shouldn't "read back" into Isaiah the notion that the servant was a divine figure. The text in Isaiah does not indicate that and we would be misreading the text to insist that it does. Nonetheless, it is entirely appropriate to use this image, as Jesus did, to gain a greater understanding of another dimension of who Jesus was and what he came to do.

In part two, then, we will mostly, but not exclusively, go back to Scripture that predates the passage we are studying for better understanding.

Part 3. Reflect (On Your Own). In part three you will find a reading that expands on one of the themes of the study. It may contain a story or commentary on the passage, or both. And it may be drawn from some other Christian author or source, whether contemporary or ancient. In any case, it is intended to help focus your mind in a single direction after the wide variety of issues raised in parts one and two. A couple of questions at the end of the reading will help you crystallize what you have learned.

Part 4. Discuss: Putting It All Together (With a Group). This part is, as the name describes, intended for group discussion. You can work through it on your own too, but some questions are repetitive with questions from the first three parts. This is intentional and necessary for group discussion; after individuals in a group have worked through each passage on their own during the week, they will want to hear from each other what they have learned and thought about. If you decide you do want to go through part four by yourself anyway, you can skip those questions that were found earlier or use those questions as opportunities to think again about key ideas. Reviewing the content is a good way for groups *and* individuals to lock

those ideas into their hearts and minds.

Groups should begin the discussion with the "Open" question and then read the passage together. Everyone will have been over the passage several times already, but reading aloud in a group can actually bring new insight.

Below are a few suggestions for group members that can facilitate rich discussion and insight:

1. Come to the study prepared. Follow the suggestions for individual study mentioned above. You will find that careful preparation will greatly enrich your time spent in group discussion.

2. Be willing to participate in the discussion. The leader of your group will not be lecturing. Instead, she or he will be asking the questions found in this guide and encouraging the members of the group to discuss what they have learned.

3. Stick to the topic being discussed. These studies focus on a particular passage of Scripture. This allows everyone to participate on equal ground and fosters in-depth study.

4. Be sensitive to the other members of the group. Listen attentively when they describe what they have learned. You may be surprised by their insights! Also note that each question assumes a variety of answers; many questions do not have "right" answers, particularly questions that aim at meaning or application. Instead the questions push us to explore the passage more thoroughly.

   When possible, link what you say to the comments of others. Also, be affirming whenever you can. This will encourage some of the more hesitant members of the group to participate.

5. Be careful not to dominate the discussion. We are sometimes so eager to express our thoughts that we leave too little opportunity for others to respond. By all means participate! But allow others to do so also.

6. Expect God to teach you through the passage being discussed and through the other members of the group. Pray that you will have an enjoyable and profitable time together, but also that as a result of the study you will find ways to take action individually and/or as a group.

7. It will be helpful for groups to follow a few basic guidelines. These guidelines, which you may wish to adapt to your situation, should be read at the beginning of the first session.

   • Anything said in the group is considered confidential and will not be discussed outside the group unless specific permission is given to do so.

   • We will provide time for each person present to talk if he or she feels comfortable doing so.

   • We will talk about ourselves and our own situations, avoiding conversation about other people.

   • We will listen attentively to each other.

   • We will be very cautious about giving advice.

Additional suggestions for the group leader can be found at the back of the guide.

Plunging into the depths of God's wisdom and love is a glorious adventure. Like Paul said in 1 Corinthians 2:9-10: "As it is written: 'What no eye has seen, what no ear has heard, and what no human mind has conceived'— the things God has prepared for those who love him—these are the things God has revealed to us by his Spirit. The Spirit searches all things, even the deep things of God." As you go in depth into Scripture, may the Spirit reveal the deep things of God's own self to you.

UNEXPECTED BLESSINGS

Matthew 5:1-12

WHERE WE'RE GOING*

The simplicity of word and profundity of thought of the Beatitudes with which the Sermon on the Mount begins have attracted each fresh generation of Christians, and many others besides. The more we explore their implications, the more seems to remain unexplored. Their wealth is inexhaustible.

Jesus spoke the Sermon on the Mount to those who were already his disciples and thereby also the citizens of God's kingdom and the children of God's family. We do not achieve this privileged status by attaining Christ's standards. Rather, by attaining his standards, or at least approximating them, we give evidence of what, by God's free grace and gift, we already are.

>   **Part 1. Investigate: Matthew 5:1-12 (On Your Own)**
>
>   **Part 2. Connect: Scripture to Scripture (On Your Own)**
>
>   **Part 3. Reflect: The People, the Qualities, the Blessings (On Your Own)**
>
>   **Part 4. Discuss: Putting It All Together (With a Group)**

A PRAYER TO PRAY

Here's a prayer you can use to set you on your way:

Creator and Redeemer, giver of all blessings, thank you for your lavish gifts to us, both spiritual and material. Though we are rebels against you and deserve only judgment from you, you freely give us your mercy in Christ. Help us as we explore the blessings which come from living as your children, so that we will better understand and be grateful for your generosity. We ask these things in the name of Jesus, who spoke these blessings. Amen.

---

*Though these studies can be used in a variety of ways and formats, for maximum benefit we recommend doing parts one, two and three on your own and then working through the questions in part four with a group.

PART 1. INVESTIGATE
Matthew 5:1-12
(On Your Own)

Read Matthew 5:1-12.

5:1-2. *Although one would stand to read Scripture publicly, Jewish teachers would sit to expound it, often with disciples sitting at their feet. Many scholars have compared the "mountain" (cf. Lk 6:17) here to Mount Sinai, where God through Moses first taught his ethics by the law (Ex 19–20; cf. Is 2:2-3).*

1. How does our normal description of the blessed or fortunate person compare with those Jesus considers blessed (vv. 1-12)?

2. To be "poor in spirit" (v. 3) is to acknowledge our spiritual poverty, our bankruptcy before God. Why is this an indispensable condition for receiving the kingdom of heaven?

Why is it so difficult for us to admit our spiritual poverty?

5:3. *Ancient writers and speakers would sometimes bracket a section of material by beginning and ending with the same phrase. These blessings thus deal with the gift of the kingdom (5:3, 10).*

Many Jewish people believed that the kingdom would be ushered in only by a great war and force of arms; Jesus promises it for the "poor in spirit," the "humble" or "meek" (5:5), the peacemakers (5:9). Poverty and piety were often associated in Judaism; the term poor *could encompass either physical poverty (Lk 6:20), or the faithful dependence on God that it often produced ("in spirit," as here).*

3. Why would those who are poor in spirit feel a need to mourn (v. 4)?

4. How do you think those who mourn will be comforted (v. 4)?

5. How would a true estimate of ourselves (vv. 3-4) lead us to be "meek"—to have a humble and gentle attitude to others (v. 5)?

6. From the world's point of view, why is it surprising that the meek will inherit the earth?

7. What has Jesus said so far that might lead us to hunger and thirst for righteousness (v. 6)?

8. Jesus promises that those who hunger and thirst for righteousness will be filled (v. 6). What can you do to cultivate a healthy, hearty spiritual appetite?

9. Jesus says the merciful will be shown mercy (v. 7). Why do you think our treatment of others will affect God's treatment of us?

10. Why would the promise of seeing God (v. 8) be reserved for those who are pure in heart?

11. Why would the world look down on the kind of people described in the Beatitudes?

12. How have the Beatitudes challenged you to be different?

Pray that you will be "blessed" in the ways Jesus promised.

5:4. *Mourning was usually associated with either repentance or bereavement; the conjunction with "comfort" means that the second aspect is in view here. It could mean grief over Israel's sins, but in this context probably refers to the pain of the oppressed. "Comfort" was one of the blessings promised for the future time when God would restore his mourning people (Is 40:1; 49:13; 51:3, 12; 52:9; 54:11; 57:18; 61:2; 66:13).*

5:5. *Here Jesus cites Scripture (Ps 37:9, 11). Not those who try to bring in the kingdom politically or militarily but those who humbly wait on God will "inherit the earth." The Hebrew of the psalm could mean "inherit the land" in a narrower sense (Ps 25:13), but in Jesus' day Jewish people expected God's people to reign over all the earth, as some other Old Testament passages suggest.*

PART 2. CONNECT
Scripture to Scripture
(On Your Own)

BLESSINGS FROM A MOUNTAIN

For a start, it is interesting to look at the setting of Jesus' discourse: "He went up on a mountainside and sat down" (v. 1). Mountains are significant throughout the Old Testament. (We should not picture something like a peak in the Rocky Mountains. Jesus was in Galilee, where the highest peak is just under four thousand feet.)

God gave Moses the Ten Commandments on Mount Sinai. In addition, once the Israelites entered Canaan, half the tribes stood on Mount Gerizim and repeated the blessings for obeying the Lord that Moses had given them, and the other half stood on Mount Ebal and proclaimed the curses for disobeying the Lord that Moses had also taught them. This happened under Joshua's leadership, but Moses was the one who had instructed them to do it (Joshua 8:33).

Similar to those mountain experiences in Israel's history, from a mountain in Galilee Jesus proclaimed his radical interpretation of the Old Testament law. And he began by pronouncing the blessings known as the Beatitudes (Matthew 5:3-12). (In Luke's version of Jesus' discourse, Jesus pronounces both blessings and woes [Luke 6:20-26], while in Matthew's account Jesus pronounces only blessings.)

OLD TESTAMENT BEATITUDES

In the Beatitudes, Jesus pronounced people with eight qualities as "blessed." The idea of declaring someone to be blessed stretches far back into the Old Testament.

Read Genesis 12:1-9.

How did the Lord promise to bless Abram (later called Abraham)?

_____

_____

_____

_____

_____

How would Abram bless the world?

_____

_____

_____

_____

In each of the following excerpts from the Psalms, someone is called "blessed." Match up the description of whomever is blessed with the reference of the psalm it comes from.

Psalm 34:8   the person who delights and meditates on the law of the Lord and does not follow the way of sinners

Psalm 41:1   the nation whose God is the Lord, whom God has chosen for his inheritance

Psalm 146:5-6   the person who takes refuge in the Lord

Psalm 1:1-3   the person who has regard for the weak

Psalm 33:12   those who dwell in the Lord's house and praise him, those whose strength is in him and whose hearts are set on pilgrimage

Psalm 84:4-5   those whose help is the Lord and whose hope is in the Lord

What similarities do you see among the various people who are called "blessed" in these psalms?

_____

_____

_____

_____

From these psalms and the passage in Genesis 12, what new insights have you gained about the meaning of being "blessed"?

_____

_____

_____

_____

THE POOR IN SPIRIT

Read Isaiah 61:1-3. Jesus quoted the first part of this passage in the synagogue in his hometown of Nazareth. What connections do you see between this passage and the first Beatitude (Matthew 5:3)? List them below.

_____

_____

_____

_____

Why do you think the gospel is "good news to the poor" (Isaiah 61:1)?

_____

_____

_____

_____

What kinds of spiritual poverty do you see around you in your everyday experience?

_____

_____

_____

_____

When and how have you seen the poor in spirit being blessed by God?

_____

_____

_____

_____

THOSE WHO MOURN

In its plainest and most familiar meaning, *mourning* is grief over some kind of profound loss. Old Testament mourning took dramatic forms. Ezekiel 27:30-32, in which the prophet predicts the fall of Tyre, lists several kinds of mourning practiced by the Israelites: "loud lamentation, putting earth on the head, rolling in ashes or dust, shaving the head, putting on sackcloth, intense weeping and chanting a lament."[1]

In Matthew 5:4, Jesus is specifically addressing mourning over sin. In the Old Testament we find several examples of people who grieve about their own sins or those of the entire nation of Israel.

Read Ezra 9:1–10:6. When the exiled Jews began to return to Jerusalem, Ezra the priest learned that they were intermarrying with the pagan people around them, a practice which God had forbidden. Even the leaders had disobeyed God in this area.

The people's sin drove Ezra into deep mourning and intense prayer. He could have kept his mourning and his prayers private. Why do you think he displayed his mourning and his grief-stricken prayers in such a public manner (9:3-6; 10:1, 6)?

_____

_____

_____

Psalm 32 is another Scripture passage that demonstrates mourning over sin and the comfort of God's forgiveness. Read Psalm 32. Note the numbers of the verses which reveal:

Mourning over sin: _____

God's comfort: _____

THE MEEK

Jesus' next Beatitude, "Blessed are the meek, for they will inherit the earth" (Matthew 5:5), is very close to Psalm 37:11. Read Psalm 37:1-11. Where do you see meekness (or humility) expressed in this passage?

_____

_____

_____

_____

In the seventh century B.C. the prophet Zephaniah foresaw the coming destruction of Jerusalem. Read Zephaniah 3:1-13.

What had gone wrong with the people and the leaders of Jerusalem?

_____

_____

_____

_____

How would the meek and humble fare in the coming destruction (vv. 12-13)?

_____

_____

_____

_____

Read 2 Kings 25:8-12, part of the account of the predicted fall of Jerusalem to the Babylonians. How was Zephaniah's prophecy about the meek and humble fulfilled?

_____

_____

_____

_____

In the Old Testament, *meekness* is a long way from *weakness*. The meek are those who humbly submit to God's will and put their lives into God's hands. Read Numbers 12:1-15. Scholar Peter Davids notes, "Moses is the chief example of a meek person (Nu. 12:3). In the story in which he is called 'meek' (or 'humble') he was being wrongly attacked by two other leaders. Instead of retaliating (after all, he had had visions and revelations from God beyond anything they had had), he humbly said nothing, not even defending himself. In the end God stepped in and defended him."[2] In the Old Testament pride was the downfall of both individuals and nations. Meanwhile God quietly kept lifting up those who humbled themselves and submitted to his will.

THOSE WHO HUNGER AND THIRST FOR RIGHTEOUSNESS

Jesus declared next, "Blessed are those who hunger and thirst for righteousness, for they will be filled" (Matthew 5:6). The theme of *righteousness* or *being righteous* pervades the Old Testament, and is applied both to God and to people. Scot McKnight writes, "Throughout Jewish literature we find two dominant ideas: God is righteous and his people are to be righteous in their behavior. The righteousness of God, primarily understood as his impeccable holiness and the conformity of his actions to that holy nature, is commonplace in Jewish thought. . . . In addition, as recent scholarship has shown, righteousness attributed to God's people refers to moral behavior conforming to God's will."[3]

Human beings have no hope of being righteous unless their Creator is first righteous. Read Psalm 71, in which the psalmist repeatedly speaks of the righteousness of God. Fill in the missing phrases for verses 15 to 19:

> My mouth will tell of _____,
>> of _____ all day long—
> though I know not how to relate them all.
> I will come and proclaim _____, Sovereign LORD;
>> I will proclaim _____, yours alone.
> Since my youth, God, you have taught me,
>> and to this day I declare your marvelous deeds.
> Even when I am old and gray,
>> do not forsake me, my God,
> till I declare your power to the next generation,
>> your mighty acts to all who are to come.
> Your _____,
>> you who have done great things.
>> Who is like you, God?

How does the writer of Psalm 71 show hunger and thirst for righteousness?

_____

_____

_____

_____

Following God's righteousness, the Old Testament also documents people who were righteous. Perhaps the most well-known example—and the first person in Scripture of whom the word *right-eousness* is used—is Abraham (called Abram here). Read Genesis 15:1-6.

Write out verse 6:

_____

_____

_____

Based on this passage and on the rest of this section on Matthew 5:5, explain in your own words what it means that Abraham had righteousness.

_____

_____

_____

THE MERCIFUL

The next Beatitude addresses the merciful: "Blessed are the merciful, for they will be shown mercy" (Matthew 5:7).

The Bible gives us evidence of God's mercy right from the start. After Adam and Eve sinned and God told them of the consequences, he demonstrated his mercy toward them immediately. Read Genesis 3. How were God's first actions after their sin acts of mercy?

_____

_____

_____

Later in the Old Testament, when the prophet Nathan confronted David about his sin of adultery with Bathsheba, David immediately confessed, "I have sinned against the LORD." Nathan instantly replied with confidence, "The LORD has taken away your sin" (2 Samuel 12:13).

David did not take God's mercy casually; he was deeply grateful for it. (Note, though, that like with Adam and Eve, there were still consequences for his sin. As Nathan predicted, Bathsheba's child died. In addition, David's family life was never harmonious after that point.) Read Psalm 51, the psalm of repentance he wrote after he committed adultery.

On what basis does David ask for mercy from God?

_____

_____

_____

What does David promise to do as a result of receiving mercy from God?

_____

_____

_____

The lesson of the depth of God's mercy stayed with David. Years later his conscience struck him because he had taken a census of Israel's warriors, an indication that he was overrelying on his military power and underrelying on God. Read 2 Samuel 24:10-14.

What were David's three choices?

_____

_____

_____

_____

Why did he decide as he did?

_____

_____

_____

_____

God's deep mercy can be irritating to those who prefer vengeance. Jonah fled when God called him to preach repentance to Nineveh. At first it looks like he was afraid or just didn't want to be inconvenienced. But read Jonah 3:1–4:11, where his true motive is revealed.

In your own words explain why Jonah was angry with God (4:1-3).

_____

_____

_____

_____

Again in your own words, restate what God said about Nineveh (4:10-11).

_____

_____

_____

_____

THE PURE IN HEART

Jesus' Beatitude in Matthew 5:8 focuses on the pure in heart, a theme that is easily seen in the Old Testament. In the instructions given to Moses for constructing the tabernacle and its furnishings, for example, *purity* is very important on every level. The gold throughout the tabernacle had to be pure gold (see Exodus 25:11, 17, 24, 29, 31, 36, 38-39). The incense burned on the altar before the Lord had to be pure incense (Exodus 30:34-35).

If building materials and physical objects used in worship had to be pure, imagine how much more important the purity of the people who came to worship God was.

Read Psalm 24. For whom do you find a beatitude, that is, a *blessing,* in this psalm?

_____

_____

_____

_____

As soon as we read Psalm 24, we recognize the problem with ourselves and with the entire human race. The writer of Proverbs 20:9 put it as a rhetorical question: "Who can say, 'I have kept my heart pure; I am clean and without sin'?" No one has the clean hands and pure heart that God requires (Psalm 24:4).

After his sin of adultery with Bathsheba, David recognized the futility of pretending that he was morally pure. His only hope for inner purity was for his heart to be changed by the Lord.

Return to Psalm 51, concentrating on verses 10-12. Write out verse 10 word for word.

_____

_____

_____

_____

How will David be able to better "see God" as a result of God's forgiveness (see vv. 12-15 especially)?

_____

_____

_____

_____

THE PEACEMAKERS

Jesus continued with his blessings: "Blessed are the peacemakers, for they will be called children of God" (Matthew 5:9). The Hebrew word *shalom,* usually translated "peace," carries a wealth of meanings. It includes the ideas of wholeness and harmony, both within a person and between people.

Read Proverbs 17:1 and restate it in your own words.

_____

_____

_____

What words and images come to mind when you hear the word *peace*? When you hear the word *strife*?

_____

_____

_____

One of the premier examples of peacemaking in the Old Testament comes in 1 Samuel 25. Read the account of how Abigail intervened with a hotheaded David to prevent an act of revenge, and then mark the following statements as true or false:

_____ David never hoped to have a peaceful relationship with Nabal.

_____ Nabal at first tried to make peace with David.

_____ Abigail went to David empty-handed.

_____ David didn't listen to Abigail because she had no authority to intervene in the situation.

_____ Abigail's intervention prevented only the death of Nabal.

_____ The Lord took care of the Nabal situation without David having to take action.

Abigail recognized that the Lord would make for David "a lasting dynasty" (1 Samuel 25:28). The Old Testament prophets consistently affirmed the permanence of David's kingdom, and they looked ahead to the ultimate king who would occupy an eternal throne.

Read Isaiah 9:6-7, part of Isaiah's prophecy about the coming king. How will peace play a role in the reign of this king?

_____

_____

_____

Isaiah confidently wrote of that future time of blessing and peace:

> The LORD's justice will dwell in the desert,
>   his righteousness live in the fertile field.
> The fruit of that righteousness will be peace;
>   its effect will be quietness and confidence forever.
> My people will live in peaceful dwelling places,
>   in secure homes,
>   in undisturbed places of rest. (Isaiah 32:16-18)

THOSE WHO ARE PERSECUTED FOR RIGHTEOUSNESS' SAKE

Jesus' eighth Beatitude is the most lengthy: "Blessed are those who are persecuted because of righteousness, for theirs is the kingdom of heaven. Blessed are you when people insult you, persecute you and falsely say all kinds of evil against you because of me. Rejoice and be glad, because great is your reward in heaven, for in the same way they persecuted the prophets who were before you" (Matthew 5:10-12).

As Jesus mentions in his last Beatitude, when the Old Testament prophets spoke the word of the Lord, their preaching seldom led to popularity.

In the first half of the eighth century B.C., the prophet Amos warned the northern kingdom of Israel that God would judge them for their idolatry, self-indulgence and complacency (Amos 2:6–7:9). The first person to speak out against Amos was a priest of the Lord, Amaziah, who should have known better. He reported Amos's words to King Jeroboam II.

Read Amos 7:10-17. Paraphrase what Amaziah said to Amos and Amos's reply.

_____

_____

_____

Despite the priest's skepticism, the northern kingdom of Israel was conquered and exiled as Amos said. Later the same judgment came to the southern kingdom of Judah. The prophet Jeremiah, among others, spoke the Lord's call to repentance. We know in some detail the abuse he suffered for speaking the word of the Lord.

Read Jeremiah 26:1-24 and mark the following statements as true or false:

_____ Jeremiah was put to death for what he had said.

_____ Priests and prophets condemned Jeremiah for saying that Jerusalem would be destroyed.

_____ Another prophet, Micah, had prophesied against Jerusalem and had been spared.

_____ Jeremiah pleaded for his life.

_____ No one stood up for Jeremiah.

_____ Another prophet, Uriah, had prophesied against Jerusalem and had been spared.

Read 2 Chronicles 36:15-16. How did the prophets serve as instruments of God's mercy?

_____

_____

_____

How would you say that the abused prophets of God were blessed?

_____

_____

_____

_____

---

[1]L. John McGregor, "Ezekiel," in *New Bible Commentary,* ed. G. J. Wenham, J. A. Motyer, D. A. Carson and R. T. France, 21st century ed. (Downers Grove, IL: InterVarsity Press, 1994), p. 733.

[2]Peter H. Davids, "James," in *New Bible Commentary,* ed. G. J. Wenham, J. A. Motyer, D. A. Carson and R. T. France, 21st century ed. (Downers Grove, IL: InterVarsity Press, 1994), p. 1362.

[3]Scot McKnight, "Justice, Righteousness," in *Dictionary of Jesus and the Gospels,* ed. Joel B. Green, Scot McKnight and I. Howard Marshall (Downers Grove, IL: InterVarsity Press, 1992), p. 412.

PART 3. REFLECT
The People, the Qualities, the Blessings
(On Your Own)

There are three general questions about Jesus' Beatitudes which need to be asked. These concern the people described, the qualities commended and the blessings promised.

THE PEOPLE DESCRIBED

The Beatitudes set forth the balanced and variegated character of Christian people. These are not eight separate and distinct groups of disciples, some of whom are meek, while others are merciful and yet others are called upon to endure persecution. They are rather eight qualities of the same group who at one and the same time are meek and merciful, poor in spirit and pure in heart, mourning and hungry, peacemakers and persecuted.

Further, the group exhibiting these marks is not an elitist set, a small spiritual aristocracy remote from the common run of Christians. On the contrary, the Beatitudes are Christ's own specification of what every Christian ought to be. All these qualities are to characterize all his followers. Unlike the gifts of the Spirit which he distributes to different members of Christ's body in order to equip them for different kinds of service, the same Spirit is concerned to work all these Christian graces in us all. There is no escape from our responsibility to covet them all.

THE QUALITIES COMMENDED

It is well known that there is at least a verbal discrepancy between the Beatitudes in Matthew's Gospel and those in Luke's. Luke writes, "Blessed are you who are poor" (Luke 6:20), while Matthew has, "Blessed are the poor in spirit." Luke's "Blessed are you who hunger now" (Luke 6:21) is recorded by Matthew as "Blessed are those who hunger and thirst for righteousness."

In consequence of this, some have argued that Luke's version is the true one, that Jesus was making a social or sociological judgment about the poor and hungry, and that Matthew spiritualized what were originally material pledges. But this is an impossible interpretation, unless we are prepared to believe either that Jesus contradicted himself or that the Gospel writers were clumsy enough to make him appear to do so. Consistently throughout his ministry Jesus repudiated the idea of establishing a material kingdom. When Pilate asked him if there was any substance in the Jewish leaders' charges against him and whether he had any political ambitions, his reply was unambiguous: "My kingdom is not of this world" (John 18:36). That is, it has a different origin and therefore a different character.

The poverty and hunger to which Jesus refers in the Beatitudes are spiritual states. It is "the poor *in spirit*" and "those who hunger and thirst *for righteousness*" whom he declares blessed. And it is safe to deduce from this that the other qualities he mentions are spiritual also.

THE BLESSINGS PROMISED

Each quality is commended, inasmuch as each person who exhibits it is pronounced "blessed." The Greek word *makarios* can and does mean "happy," and several commentators have explained them as Jesus' prescription for human happiness. There is no need to dismiss this interpretation as entirely fallacious. For nobody knows better than our Creator how we may become truly human beings. He made us. He knows how we work best. All Christians can testify from experience that there is a close connection between holiness and happiness.

Nevertheless, it is seriously misleading to

render *makarios* as "happy." For happiness is a subjective state, whereas Jesus is making an objective judgment about these people. He is declaring not what they may feel like ("happy") but what God thinks of them and what on that account they are: they are "blessed."

What is this blessing? The second half of each Beatitude elucidates it. They possess the kingdom of heaven and they inherit the earth. The mourners are comforted and the hungry are satisfied. They receive mercy, they see God, they are called the children of God. Their heavenly reward is great. And all these blessings belong together. Just as the eight qualities describe every Christian (at least in the ideal), so the eight blessings are given to every Christian. These eight qualities together constitute the responsibilities, and the eight blessings the privileges, of being a citizen of God's kingdom. This is what the enjoyment of God's rule means.

Are these blessings present or future? Personally, I think the only possible answer is "both." Some commentators have insisted that they are future, and have emphasized the eschatological nature of the Beatitudes. Certainly the second part of the last Beatitude promises the persecuted a great reward in heaven, and this must be future. Nevertheless, it is plain from the rest of Jesus' teaching that the kingdom of God is a present reality which we can receive, inherit or enter now. Similarly, we can obtain mercy and comfort now, can become God's children now, and in this life can have our hunger satisfied and our thirst quenched. Jesus promised all these blessings to his followers in the here and now. So then the promises of Jesus in the Beatitudes have both a present and a future fulfillment. We enjoy the firstfruits now; the full harvest is yet to come.

What's the main idea in this section?

What is one thing you can act on based on this reading?

PART 4. DISCUSS
Putting It All Together
(With a Group)

OPEN

Whom do you normally consider to be blessed or fortunate?

READ MATTHEW 5:1-12.

A hymn by William Cowper reminds us to look for blessings in unexpected places.

> You fearful saints, fresh courage take;
> The clouds you so much dread
> Are big with mercy, and shall break
> In blessings on your head.

Jesus' Beatitudes set forth the blessings which God bestows, not as a reward for merit but as a gift of grace upon those in whom he is forming a Christlike character.

1. What general statements can you make about the kind of people Jesus pronounces as blessed?

2. Which of the Beatitudes focus on a Christian's relationship with God?

3. Which of the Beatitudes focus on a Christian's relationship with other people?

4. From "Connect: Scripture to Scripture," who are some people in the Old Testament (named and unnamed) who are called *blessed*?

5. How are the blessings of Matthew 5:1-12 both present and future?

6. When have you been most aware that you were *poor in spirit*?

7. Those who *mourn* feel sorrow not only for their own sin but also for the sin they see around them. What have you heard in the news lately that causes you to mourn?

8. What's the most powerful example of meekness that you've seen?

9. Biblical righteousness has three aspects: legal, moral and social. What does it mean to hunger and thirst for each of these?

10. What steps can you take to develop a more robust *hunger and thirst for righteousness* in these different areas?

11. When has receiving mercy encouraged you to be merciful?

12. What attitudes and practices move us toward purity?

13. Where do you wish you could be a *peacemaker*? What steps do you need to take for that to happen?

14. How can you encourage someone who is being *persecuted for the sake of Christ*?

Jesus' entire Sermon on the Mount portrays the repentance and the righteousness which belong to the kingdom of God. That is, it describes what human life and human community look like when they come under the gracious rule of God. And what do they look like? Different! Jesus' followers are to be entirely different from others.

No doubt the Beatitudes have challenged you to be different. Pray that you will be open to the Holy Spirit, and that the Spirit will bring about the changes that need to be made.

SESSION TWO

God's Way to Make a Difference

Matthew 5:13-16

WHERE WE'RE GOING

Word-pictures are powerful, and people respond best to images which are closest to home. A familiar word-picture involves people's senses, so that they instantly see, feel, hear, smell, even taste the speaker's words. When Jesus spoke to his followers about their influence on society, he did not use abstract terms. He used two very familiar everyday images: salt and light.

Part 1. Investigate: Matthew 5:13-16 (On Your Own)

Part 2. Connect: Scripture to Scripture (On Your Own)

Part 3. Reflect: Two Domestic Metaphors (On Your Own)

Part 4. Discuss: Putting It All Together (With a Group)

A PRAYER TO PRAY

Here's a prayer you can use to set you on your way:

Jesus, light of the world, thank you for revealing yourself to us, illuminating our path to you and then illuminating our paths through life. You shine your truth on us and you preserve us in the midst of evil. We ask that you give us grace not to grasp you to ourselves in selfishness or fear, but to be bold to influence those around us for you. During this study, bring to our minds specific ways we can be salt and light in the world so that others will give you glory. Amen.

PART 1. INVESTIGATE
Matthew 5:13-16

Read Matthew 5:13-16.

5:13-16. *A disciple of the kingdom who does not live like a disciple of the kingdom (5:3-12) is worth about as much as tasteless salt or invisible light.*

5:13. *Various scholars have emphasized different uses of salt in antiquity, such as a preservative or an agent regularly added to manure; but the use of salt here is as a flavoring agent: "if salt has become tasteless" (the Greek word can also mean "become foolish," so it may include a play on words).*

Although the salt recovered from impure salt substances taken from the Dead Sea could dissolve, leaving only the impurities behind, the point here is closer to that expressed by a rabbi at the end of the first century. When asked how one could make saltless salt salty again, he replied that one should salt it with the afterbirth of a mule. Being sterile, mules have no afterbirth, and he was saying that those who ask a stupid question receive a stupid answer. Real salt does not lose its saltiness; but if it did, what would you do to restore its salty flavor—salt it? Unsalty salt was worthless.

1. What positive qualities of salt and light do you think Jesus had in mind as he spoke these words?

2. Before refrigeration, salt was used to keep meat from rotting. What then does Jesus' statement "You are the salt of the earth" (v. 13) tell us about society and the church's role in it?

3. What has been in the news lately that indicates society is rotting and decaying?

4. What are some practical ways we can function as salt where we live and work (v. 13)?

5. What might cause Christians to lose their saltiness (v. 13)?

6. Jesus' second statement is "You are the light of the world" (v. 14). As salt we prevent decay, the spread of evil. How does the church's role as light complement its role as salt?

7. How can we positively promote the spread of truth in the world?

8. Why might we be tempted to hide our light (v. 15)?

5:14. *Jewish tradition considered Israel (Is 42:6; 49:6) and Jerusalem (as well as God and the law) the light of the world. The "city" here may thus be Jerusalem; or it may be any elevated city at night, whose torch lights would make it visible to the surrounding countryside.*

9. What is the result, according to Jesus, of people seeing our good deeds (v. 16)?

10. What examples can you think of where the work of Christians has brought people closer to God?

5:15-16. *The small wicker oil lamps of this period gave little light in the average home, which had few windows; they would be most effective by being set on a lampstand. Something large placed over them would presumably extinguish the light altogether.*

11. What relationship do you see between the Beatitudes and our role as salt and light in society?

12. What is one way you can begin having a stronger influence as salt and as light?

Pray for the areas of rottenness in our world and for your ability to shine the light of truth.

PART 2. CONNECT
Scripture to Scripture

SALT

Matthew 5 is certainly not the first mention of salt in Scripture. Scholars point out, "The Bible's writers made generous use of salt imagery, sprinkling references to its use and abuse throughout Scripture, particularly in the OT. Biblical writers are well aware of salt's properties, associating it with images of seasoning, preserving and purifying—or with powerful images of death, desolation and curse."[1]

In his declaration "You are the salt of the earth," Jesus obviously meant "salt" to convey a positive meaning. Jesus' phrase is firmly established in English as a complimentary assessment of a person's character. To call someone "the salt of the earth" is to praise the person for being honest, humble, dependable and without pretense.

A look at what salt symbolizes in the Old Testament, however, shows us that when Jesus said, "You are the salt of the earth," he meant more than "You are honest unpretentious people"—although the meaning could include those qualities.

Salt played a symbolic role in Old Testament sacrifices. Read Leviticus 2:11-13. How was salt involved in grain offerings to the Lord?

_____

_____

_____

_____

"The salt of the covenant of your God" (Leviticus 2:13) is a mysterious phrase. Other Scriptures give us a clue to the meaning of the words.

Read Numbers 18:14-19, where God speaks to Aaron about the rights and responsibilities of the priests and Levites, and 2 Chronicles 13:1-7. Fill in the missing phrases:

Numbers 18:19: "Whatever is set aside from the holy offerings the Israelites present to the LORD I give to you and your sons and daughters as your perpetual share. It is _____

_____ for both you and your offspring."

2 Chronicles 13:5: "Don't you know that the LORD, the God of Israel, has given the kingship of Israel to David and his descendants _____?"

Because salt acts as a preservative, it symbolizes *permanence*: "References to the covenant of salt capitalize on salt's preserving qualities as symbolic of a permanent indissoluble relationship between God and his people (Lev 2:13; Num 18:19; 2 Chron 13:5). Likewise, salt is listed as a required addition to all burnt offerings because of its preserving qualities (Ezra 6:9)."[2]

Even in places where salt is not specifically mentioned in Scripture, we can see evidence of the metaphor, like in 2 Samuel. Once King David had established himself in Jerusalem and built himself a comfortable cedar palace, he began to feel guilty that the Ark of the Covenant was still housed in a portable tent made of fabric and animal skins. He resolved to build a permanent temple for the Lord. The prophet Nathan agreed at first, until he received a contradictory message from God. Read 2 Samuel 7:1-17.

No salt was mentioned when God promised, "Your house and your kingdom will endure forever before me; your throne will be established forever" (2 Samuel 7:16), but what is it about God's covenant with David that would make it a "covenant of salt" (2 Chronicles 13:5)?

_____

_____

_____

_____

Salt in the Old Testament also had connotations of *new beginnings* or *separation.*

"Newborn babies were rubbed with salt: 'On the day you were born your cord was not cut, nor were you washed with water to make you clean, nor were you rubbed with salt or wrapped in cloths' (Ezek 16:4 NIV). To Abimelech, spreading salt on a captured city symbolized a curse: he 'razed the city and sowed it with salt' (Judg 9:45 NASB). Salt in the soil would inhibit the growth of food crops, but also it symbolized a break from the past. When Elisha treated a bad water supply at Jericho with salt, it may have symbolized a new beginning in terms of removing the curse Joshua had leveled on it: 'And he went out to the spring of water, and threw salt in it and said, "Thus says the LORD, 'I have purified these waters'"' (2 Kings 2:21)."[3]

The midwife attending a birth would typically cleanse the newborn baby's skin with salt. A baby *not* cleansed with salt is the image of an abandoned child, while the child cleansed with salt is welcomed and is given a good start in life.

The prophet Elisha's purifying of the water supply of Jericho was his first act as successor to Elijah. In that sense he not only made the water useable but demonstrated the fresh beginnings of his prophetic ministry. We normally think that adding salt to water makes it undrinkable, but the amount of salt in Elisha's "new bowl" would be trivial compared to Jericho's water supply.

Abimelech, with the support of the citizens of Shechem, murdered his seventy brothers and established himself as ruler over Israel. Three years later enmity arose between Abimelech and Shechem, and he attempted to wipe out Shechem forever, scattering salt over the site of the city as a symbol of its destruction. Shortly afterward Abimelech himself was killed at Thebes, where some of the citizens of Shechem had fled.

LIGHT AND LAMPS

In a scene of great drama, Genesis 1 relates the creation of light where there had been only darkness: "And God said, 'Let there be light,' and there was light. God saw that the light was good, and he separated the light from the darkness" (Genesis 1:3-4). Sun, moon and stars followed: "God made two great lights—the greater light to govern the day and the lesser light to govern the night. He also made the stars. God set them in the vault of the sky to give light on the earth, to govern the day and the night, and to separate light from darkness. And God saw that it was good" (Genesis 1:16-18). Without the creation of the sun around which our solar system revolves, human life—as we know it—would not be possible.

When Jesus said, "You are the light of the world," however, he was not referring to the natural light of the sun, moon or stars. He was talking about something closer to home, something every one of his hearers (except the blind) understood: lights in the windows of buildings, lights in cities, lights in houses. Those listening in would most likely have thought of the oil lamps that illumined their own homes. Scholar Robin Nixon gives us a more detailed picture:

> Lamps could be held in the hand, set on a shelf or placed on a stand. . . . A simple wooden stand would serve most households, but some Iron Age lamps were provided with thick bases or separate hollow pedestals. Where brighter light was needed lamps with several spouts were employed, seven-spouted examples having been found in Palestine from this and earlier times, and many with provision for multiple wicks are known from the Roman era.[4]

Household lamps are used metaphorically throughout Scripture. Read the following verses that mention lamps and match the reference on the left with what each lamp symbolizes in those verses:

Psalm 119:105	parents' commands to their children
Proverbs 6:20-23	a descendant in David's line
Proverbs 20:27	the Lord himself
1 Kings 15:1-4	the human spirit
2 Samuel 22:29	God's word

How is each item in the right column a source of "light"?

_____

_____

_____

_____

Fallen humanity is in spiritual darkness and can be truly enlightened only by the Holy Spirit. Read Psalm 36:5-9. Write out verse 9 word for word:

_____

_____

_____

_____

In your own words, how would you explain the statement "in your light we see light"?

_____

_____

_____

_____

LIGHT IN ISRAEL'S HISTORY

Besides the metaphorical meanings of *light*, actual physical light came into play at dramatic moments in Israel's history. Of all the plagues that came on Egypt, perhaps the most terrifying—at least before the final slaying of the firstborn—was the three-day plague of darkness. Read Exodus 10:21-23. During the plague, how could the Egyptians and the Israelites be differentiated?

_____

_____

_____

_____

Light from God was also vital to Israel during the exodus from Egypt. Read Exodus 13:20-22. From your own imagination, sketch what you think this divine guidance looked like:

Surely the psalmist was thinking of God's guidance for Israel through the desert trek to Mount Sinai when he wrote:

> Send me your light and your faithful care,
> > let them lead me;
> let them bring me to your holy mountain,
> > to the place where you dwell. (Psalm 43:3)

How would you describe the differences between people led by the light of God and those not led in this way?

_____

_____

_____

_____

THE LIGHT OF THE MESSIAH

Two great passages about the coming Messiah are found in Isaiah, chapters 42 and 49. Read Isaiah 42:1-7 and Isaiah 49:1-7. Write out what is said in both passages about *light*:

_____

_____

_____

_____

_____

The Messiah will not only *bring* light to the Gentiles; he will *be* a light to the Gentiles. All the positive properties of lamps and firelight will reside in him.

Israel itself was called by God to be a light to the rest of the world—the Gentiles. Read Isaiah 60:1-7. When Israel reflects the glory of God, what will be the results for the "nations," that is, the Gentile world?

_____

_____

_____

_____

_____

---

[1]Leland Ryken, James C. Wilhoit and Tremper Longman, eds., "Salt," in *Dictionary of Biblical Imagery* (Downers Grove, IL: InterVarsity Press, 1998), p. 752.

[2]Ibid.

[3]Ibid.

[4]Robin E. Nixon, "Lamp, Lampstand, Lantern," in *New Bible Dictionary,* ed. I. Howard Marshall, A. R. Millard, J. I. Packer and D. J. Wiseman, 3rd ed. (Downers Grove, IL: InterVarsity Press, 1996), p. 663.

PART 3. REFLECT
Two Domestic Metaphors

If the Beatitudes describe the essential character of the disciples of Jesus, the salt and light metaphors indicate their influence for good in the world. Yet the very notion that Christians can exert a healthy influence in the world should bring us up with a start. What possible influence could the people described in the Beatitudes exert in this hard, tough world?

Jesus did not share this skepticism. He referred to that handful of Palestinian peasants as the salt of *the earth* and the light of *the world,* so far-reaching was their influence to be. It is also a remarkable providence of God that in Matthew, the most Jewish of the four Gospels, there should be such an allusion to the whole earth, to the worldwide power for good of Christ's followers.

In order to define the nature of their influence, Jesus resorted to two domestic metaphors. Every home, however poor, used and still uses both salt and light. The need for light is obvious. Salt, on the other hand, had a variety of uses. It was both a condiment and a preservative. It seems to have been recognized from time immemorial as an essential component of human diet and as a seasoning or relish to food.

The basic truth which lies behind these metaphors and is common to them both is that the church and the world are distinct communities. On the one hand there is "the earth"; on the other there is "you" who are the earth's salt. On the one hand there is "the world"; on the other there is "you" who are the world's light.

Jesus' metaphors tell us something about both communities. The world is evidently a dark place with little or no light of its own, since an external source of light is needed to illumine it. The world also manifests a constant tendency to deteriorate. It cannot stop itself from going bad. Only salt introduced from outside can do this.

When we look at the two metaphors more closely, we see that they are deliberately phrased in order to be parallel to each other. In each case Jesus first makes an affirmation ("You are the salt of the earth," "You are the light of the world"). Then he adds a rider, the condition on which the affirmation depends (the salt must retain its saltiness, the light must be allowed to shine). Salt is good for nothing if its saltiness is lost; light is good for nothing if it is concealed.

When each community is itself and is true to itself, the world decays like rotten fish or meat, while the church can hinder its decay. Of course God has established certain institutions in his common grace, which curb humanity's sinful tendencies and prevent society from slipping into anarchy. Nevertheless, God intends the most powerful of all restraints within sinful society to be his own redeemed, regenerate and righteous people.

The effect of salt, however, is conditional: it must retain its saltiness. Now strictly speaking, salt can never lose its saltiness. Nevertheless, it can become contaminated by mixture with impurities, and then become useless, even dangerous. Dr. David Turk suggested to me that what was then popularly called "salt" was in fact a white powder (perhaps from around the Dead Sea) which, while containing sodium chloride, also contained much else. Of this dust the sodium chloride was probably the most soluble component and so the most easily washed out. The residue of white powder still looked like salt, and was doubtless still called salt, but it neither tasted nor acted like salt. It was just road dust.

So too a Christian. Christian saltiness is

Christian character as depicted in the Beatitudes, committed Christian discipleship exemplified in both deed and word. For effectiveness the Christian must retain his Christlikeness, as salt must retain its saltness. The influence of Christians in and on society depends on their being distinct, not identical.

Jesus introduces his second metaphor with a similar affirmation: "You are the light of the world." What this light is Jesus clarifies as our "good deeds." Let people once "see your good deeds," he said, and they will "glorify your Father in heaven," for it is by such good deeds that our light is to shine (Matthew 5:16). It seems that "good deeds" is a general expression to cover everything a Christian says and does because he or she is a Christian, every outward and visible manifestation of a person's Christian faith.

Since light is a common biblical symbol of truth, a Christian's shining light must surely include spoken testimony. Evangelism must be counted as one of the good deeds by which our light shines and our Father is glorified. It is healthy to be reminded that believing, confessing and teaching the truth are good deeds which give evidence of our regeneration by the Holy Spirit. We must not limit them to these, however.

"Good deeds" are works of love as well as of faith. They express not only our loyalty to God, but our care for our fellows as well. Indeed, the primary meaning of "deeds" must be practical, visible works of compassion. It is when people see these, Jesus said, that they will glorify God, for they embody the good news of his love which we proclaim. Without them our gospel loses its credibility and our God his honor.

As with the salt, so with the light; the affirmation is followed by a condition: "let your light shine before others" (v. 16). We are not to be like a town or village nestling in a valley whose lights are concealed from view, but like a "town built on a hill" which "cannot be hidden" and whose lights are clearly seen for miles around (v. 14). Again, we are to be like a lighted lamp, which is set on a lampstand in a prominent position in the house so that "it gives light to everyone in the house" and is not stuck under a bowl where it can do no good (v. 15).

That is, as the disciples of Jesus, we are not to conceal the truth we know or the truth of what we are. We are not to pretend to be other than we are, but be willing for our Christianity to be visible to all. Then people will see us and our good deeds, and seeing us will glorify God. For they will inevitably recognize that it is by the grace of God we are what we are, that *our* light is *his* light, and that our works are his works done in us and through us.

The salt and light metaphors which Jesus used have much to teach us about our Christian responsibilities in the world. Three lessons are prominent.

First, there is a fundamental difference between Christians and non-Christians, between the church and the world. This theme is basic to the Sermon on the Mount. The Sermon is built on the assumption that Christians *are* different, and it issues a call to us to *be* different.

Second, we must accept the responsibility which this distinction puts upon us. It is when in each metaphor we bring the affirmation and the condition together that our responsibility stands out. Each affirmation begins in the Greek sentence with the emphatic pronoun "you," as much as to say "you and only you" are the earth's salt and the world's light. And *therefore*—the condition follows with inexorable logic—you simply must not fail the world you are called to serve.

Third, we must see our Christian responsibility as twofold. The function of salt is largely negative: it prevents decay. The function of light is positive: it illumines the darkness. So Jesus calls his disciples to exert a double influence on the secular community, a negative influence by arresting its decay and a positive influence by bringing light into its darkness. For it is one thing to stop the spread of evil; it is another to promote the spread of truth, beauty and goodness. We should never put Christian social and evangelistic responsibilities over against each other as if we had to choose between them. If we neglect either responsibility, we will be guilty of separating what Jesus has united.

What's the main idea in this section?

What is one thing you can act on based on this reading?

PART 4. DISCUSS
Putting It All Together

OPEN

There are people in the world who never open a Bible. Still, they are forming impressions about God every time they meet a Christian. You may be the only Bible that someone will read. Think about someone who has been like a Bible for you, showing in their life what God is like. What did that person say or do that showed God to you?

READ MATTHEW 5:13-16.

In the Beatitudes Jesus congratulates those whom the world most pities, and he calls the world's rejects "blessed." Now he tells those blessed people that they are the world's greatest influence for good.

1. What did you find out about the functions of salt in biblical times?

2. From part two, what did you learn about the significance of a "covenant of salt"?

3. What are some ways Christians function as "salt" in society?

4. The reading mentions that the white powder called "salt" in biblical times could lose its actual salt but still look like salt. What might cause Christians to lose their saltiness (v. 13)?

5. What did you learn from "Connect: Scripture to Scripture" about the symbolism of lamps in the Old Testament?

6. The image of putting a lamp under a bowl (v. 15) is laughable. It's easy to wonder why somebody would do that. But what are some "bowls" under which Christians hide their light?

7. Think of areas where our society is the most "rotten." How can you have an influence for Christ in one of those areas?

8. Compare your Christian life now with how it was several years ago (or, if you are a new believer, some shorter length of time ago). Would you say you have become more "salty" or less, and why?

9. When have you been bold to let your light shine, and why?

10. When have you preferred to hide your light, and why?

11. What examples can you think of where the work of Christians has motivated people to praise God—or at least consider him in a new way?

12. Where do you most long to see the light of Christ shine into darkness?

Pray that you—the salt of the earth and the light of the world—will affect others for good through the Holy Spirit, and that you will not lose your saltiness or hide your light.

SESSION THREE

The Importance of Obeying God's Law

Matthew 5:17-20

WHERE WE'RE GOING

Jesus now explains that the righteousness he has already mentioned twice as that for which his disciples hunger (v. 6) and on account of which they suffer (v. 10) is a conformity to God's moral law and yet surpasses the righteousness of the scribes and Pharisees (v. 20). The "good deeds" (v. 16) are works of obedience. He began his sermon with beatitudes in the third person ("Blessed are the poor in spirit"); he continued in the second person ("You are the salt of the earth"); and now he changes to the authoritative first person and uses for the first time his distinctive and dogmatic formula *I tell you* (vv. 18-20).

Part 1. Investigate: Matthew 5:17-20 (On Your Own)

Part 2. Connect: Scripture to Scripture (On Your Own)

Part 3. Reflect: As Enduring as the Universe (On Your Own)

Part 4. Discuss: Putting It All Together (With a Group)

A PRAYER TO PRAY

Here's a prayer you can use to set you on your way:

Father in heaven, gracious giver of the law, we thank you for communicating to us what is right and good. You have not left us to flounder around and guess at what righteousness looks like and acts like. You have told us, and you have shown us in Jesus Christ. We pray with the psalmist, "Open my eyes that I may see wonderful things in your law" so that we will believe and obey you. We ask this in the name of Jesus who fulfilled all the law. Amen.

PART 1. INVESTIGATE
Matthew 5:17-20

Read Matthew 5:17-20.

1. This passage naturally divides into two parts, verses 17-18 and verses 19-20. What does each part emphasize?

5:17. *Jewish teachers said that one "abolished" the law by disobeying it (cf. Deut 27:26), because one thereby rejected its authority. Such highhanded rebellion against the law—as opposed to particular sins—warranted social and spiritual expulsion from the Jewish community. The charge of openly persuading others that the law was no longer in force would be even worse. Jesus opposed not the law but an illegitimate interpretation of it that stressed regulations more than character.*

2. Why might some people have thought that Jesus came to abolish the Law and the Prophets (v. 17)?

3. The Law and the Prophets (the Old Testament) consist of doctrine, prophecy and ethical precepts. In what sense has Jesus fulfilled each of these (v. 17)?

4. How does Jesus emphasize his high view of Old Testament Scripture (vv. 17-18)?

5:18. *Jesus refers here to the yod, the smallest letter in the Hebrew alphabet. Later rabbis told the story that when God changed Sarai's name to Sarah, the yod that was removed complained to God for generations till he reinserted it, this time in Joshua's name. Jewish teachers used illustrations like this to make the point that the law was sacred and one could not regard any part as too small to be worth keeping.*

How can Jesus' words strengthen our confidence in Scripture?

5. What portions of the Bible have you tended to skip over or neglect?

How can you make studying these a higher priority?

6. How will our response to the Old Testament law determine our status in the kingdom of heaven (v. 19)?

7. The Pharisees and teachers of the law were zealous about observing the law. How can our righteousness possibly surpass theirs (v. 20)?

5:20. *The Pharisees were the most respected religious people of the day, and the scribes the supreme experts in the law (especially, no doubt, the Pharisaic scribes). Verses 21-48 show what Jesus' demand for a "higher" righteousness involves. The Pharisees also stressed the right intention of the heart* (kavanah); *Jesus criticizes not their doctrine but their hearts as religious people. Religious communities led by Pharisaic teachers may have also been opponents of Jewish Christians in Syria-Palestine in Matthew's day, giving Matthew additional incentive to record these words.*

8. Jesus states that only those who have this surpassing righteousness will enter the kingdom of heaven (v. 20). How can this be harmonized with his statement about the poor in spirit (those who admit their spiritual bankruptcy) entering the kingdom (5:3)?

9. Some people claim that Jesus abolished the Old Testament law for the Christian and that we are only responsible for obeying the "law of love." Respond to this view in light of Jesus' words in this passage.

10. How should you study and apply the Old Testament law today?

Pray that you will receive new spiritual insight as you continue to study the Bible.

PART 2. CONNECT
Scripture to Scripture

THE LAW AND THE PROPHETS

What is this "Law" and "Prophets" which Jesus did not come to abolish but to fulfill?

The Hebrew Scriptures (which we call the Old Testament) are divided into the Law, the Prophets and the Writings. The *Law* is the Pentateuch, the first five books of the Bible: Genesis, Exodus, Leviticus, Numbers and Deuteronomy. The *Prophets* are the major prophets (Joshua, Judges, the books of Samuel, the books of Kings, Isaiah, Jeremiah, Ezekiel and Daniel) and the minor prophets (the final twelve books of the Old Testament), designated as major and minor because of their length rather than their relative importance. The phrase "the Law and the Prophets" came to stand in for the whole of Hebrew Scripture.

The Pentateuch is also called the Torah. Scholars tell us that "a survey of the 220 occurrences of *tôrâ* [Torah] throughout the OT reveals three main aspects to this word. It involves (1) teaching or instruction to be learned, (2) commands to be obeyed and (3) guidance about how to live in specific situations. These meanings can be distinguished by the verbs associated with *tôrâ*, by the context of those addressed and by the responses expected."[1]

One of the central events of Israel's history is the giving of the Ten Commandments, or the "ten words," at Mount Sinai, which happened in connection with the exodus from Egypt. Long before that time, however, God had clearly communicated some aspects of his will to humanity and, more specifically, to the descendants of Abraham.

Read Genesis 2:15–3:3. What law did God communicate to the first humans, and with what consequences for disobedience?

_____

_____

_____

_____

_____

Read Genesis 39:1-10. What law had God clearly communicated to Joseph at some point?

_____

_____

_____

_____

_____

Read Exodus 18:13-23. When Moses' father-in-law, Jethro, came to visit the Israelite encampment in the desert, they were near Mount Sinai but had not yet received the Ten Commandments from the Lord. What is said here about God's "decrees and instructions" (vv. 16, 20)?

_____

_____

_____

_____

THE GIVING OF THE TEN COMMANDMENTS

Whatever and however the Lord had already communicated to people about his will, the pinnacle of his law-giving occurred on Mount Sinai in the third month after the Israelites left Egypt. Read Exodus 19 and 20. Respond to the following questions as true or false:

_____ The people promised to obey the Lord.

_____ Only Moses heard the voice of the Lord.

_____ God's covenant depended on obedience.

_____ The scene included fire, smoke and a trumpet blast.

_____ God was angry because the people took his presence too casually.

_____ The Lord told Moses not to bring anyone up the mountain with him.

Fill in the missing portions of these verses from the Ten Commandments in Exodus 20:

You shall have _____ before me. (v. 3)

You shall not make for yourself _____ in heaven above or on the earth beneath or in the waters below. You shall not _____. (vv. 4-5)

You shall not _____ of the LORD your God. (v. 7)

Remember the _____ holy. Six days you shall labor and do all your work, but the seventh day is _____. (vv. 8-10)

Honor _____, so that you may _____ the LORD your God is giving you. (v. 12)

You shall _____. (v. 13)

You shall not _____. (v. 14)

You shall _____. (v. 15)

You shall not give _____ neighbor. (v. 16)

You shall not covet _____ or his male or female servant, his ox or donkey, or _____ your neighbor. (v. 17)

If all these commandments were obeyed, what kind of society would result? Use all the descriptive words you can think of.

_____

_____

_____

_____

The rest of Exodus, all of Leviticus and much of Numbers are made up of laws which are an elaboration of the Ten Commandments. The book of Deuteronomy is a retelling of the giving of the law and further elaboration on it.

The Ten Commandments were originally written on two tablets of stone "inscribed on both sides, front and back. The tablets were the work of God; the writing was the writing of God, engraved on the tablets" (Exodus 32:15-16). Scholar Martin Selman points out the significance of this: "What chiefly differentiates the Ten Commandments from other forms of *tôrâ* is that they were given directly by God rather than through any human agency. They were uniquely written on two stone tablets by 'the finger of God' (Ex 31:18), and the law-giving was accompanied by a dramatic theophany. . . . The fact that Yahweh gave the commandments to those he had freed from slavery in Egypt (Ex 20:1-2; Deut 5:6) emphasizes how closely they are bound up with the person and presence of a redeeming, liberating God."[2]

Despite the glory happening at the top of Mount Sinai, the Israelites at the foot of the mountain grew impatient waiting for Moses, and with Aaron's acquiescence they began to worship an idol and carouse. When Moses returned, he furiously threw down the tablets and broke them.

After a crisis of intercession and repentance, Moses was given two new stone tablets for the Ten Commandments (Exodus 34:1, 27-28). When Moses came down from the mountain with the new stone tablets, something dramatic had happened.

Read Exodus 34:29-35. Describe in your own words the change that had come over Moses and what happened as a result.

_____

_____

_____

_____

The stone tablets were placed in the most holy of sites, the Ark of the Covenant, which resided within the Holy of Holies in the tabernacle (Exodus 25:16; 40:20).

OBEDIENCE AND DISOBEDIENCE

The Israelites entered Canaan and later were ruled by three kings in succession: Saul, David and Solomon. After Solomon's death in 930 B.C. the kingdom was torn in two and became the southern kingdom of Judah and the northern kingdom of Israel. Judah had a succession of kings, some faithful to the Lord, some idolaters. King Hezekiah held fast to the Lord and took the initiative to destroy idolatry in Judah. During his reign Assyria conquered the northern kingdom of Israel, but God miraculously saved Judah (including Jerusalem; see 2 Kings 18–20).

Hezekiah's son Manasseh went in the opposite direction, doing "evil in the eyes of the LORD, following the detestable practices of the nations the LORD had driven out before the Israelites" (2 Kings 21:2). In the most audacious display of idolatry, Manasseh built pagan altars right inside the Lord's temple: "In the two courts of the temple of the LORD, he built altars to all the starry hosts" (2 Kings 21:5). When the king of Assyria temporarily took him prisoner, Manasseh had a change of heart, but it did not carry over to his son Amon, who reigned next. Amon "did evil in the eyes of the LORD, as his father Manasseh had done. He followed completely the ways of his father, worshiping the idols his father had worshiped, and bowing down to them. He forsook the LORD, the God of his ancestors, and did not walk in obedience to him" (2 Kings 21:20-22). Amon was assassinated, and then his assassins were assassinated, so Amon's son Josiah became king of Judah.

By this time worship of the Lord had so deteriorated that the land of Judah was littered with shrines to various idols. The temple in Jerusalem was still defiled with idolatrous altars. Years of neglect had also filled the temple with general debris. So neglected were the temple and God's laws that the Book of the Law—the scrolls of the Torah—had gone missing among the temple rubble.

King Josiah was different from his predecessors, however. Scripture tells us that "Josiah was eight years old when he became king, and he reigned in Jerusalem thirty-one years. He did what was right in the eyes of the LORD and followed the ways of his father David, not turning aside to the right or to the left. In the eighth year of his reign, while he was still young, he began to seek the God of his father David. In his twelfth year he began to purge Judah and Jerusalem of high places, Asherah poles and idols" (2 Chronicles 34:1-3).

At age twenty Josiah started a massive purification and repair of God's temple. Read 2 Chronicles 34:14-33. Choose the correct answer for each of the following statements:

During the work in the temple, Hilkiah the priest found the Book of the Law and
___ a. took it to Josiah.
___ b. read it to Josiah.
___ c. gave it to Shaphan the secretary.
___ d. hid it.
___ e. copied it for Josiah.

When words of the law were read to Josiah, he immediately
___ a. refused to listen.
___ b. took a knife, cut off pieces of the scroll and burned them.
___ c. sent it back to its proper place in the temple.
___ d. was shocked and tore his robes.
___ e. asked for it to be read to him a second time.

Hilkiah the priest consulted Huldah the prophetess, who
___ a. sent the scroll back immediately.
___ b. expressed the Lord's pleasure toward Josiah for humbling himself.
___ c. predicted good times ahead for Judah because of the people's repentance.
___ d. asked to have some of the scroll read in her presence.
___ e. commended Hilkiah for asking her advice.

Josiah himself read the law to the elders of Judah and Jerusalem and
___ a. repented of his own idolatry.
___ b. called for trumpets to be sounded.
___ c. renewed the covenant and promised to follow the Lord's commandments.
___ d. led the people in weeping and repentance.
___ e. predicted the fall of Jerusalem.

Sadly the dramatic reforms under Josiah did not last. Less than fifty years after his reign, in 586 B.C., the Babylonians conquered Jerusalem, burned the temple and took masses of people into exile. The Jews began to return from Babylon only after the Persians had taken over from the Babylonians. King Cyrus of Persia issued a proclamation allowing the Jews to return (2 Chronicles 36:22-23).

The temple was in ruins, but during the years of the Babylonian exile, the law had been preserved. Read Ezra 7:1-10. Write out verse 10:

_____

_____

_____

_____

_____

The temple of Jerusalem was rebuilt, although not to the grandeur of Solomon's temple. Now the next step was to renew the people's commitment to God's law. Read Nehemiah 7:73–8:10. Describe the scene as Ezra read the law aloud. What would people have seen, heard, felt, smelled and tasted?

_____

_____

_____

_____

_____

Why do you think the people wept when they heard the law (v. 9)?

_____

_____

_____

_____

_____

How were the people told to respond to the law once they were dismissed (vv. 10-12)?

_____

_____

_____

_____

_____

Why do you think they were to respond in that way?

_____

_____

_____

_____

_____

THE RICHES OF THE LAW

Read Psalm 19. Verses 7-11 burst out in poetic praise for God's law. Find the correct verse numbers for what is said about God's law (noted sometimes as singular and sometimes as plural ["laws"]):

_____ are right

_____ are radiant

_____ are more precious than gold

_____ refreshes the soul

_____ give warning

_____ gives joy

_____ are firm

_____ are sweeter than honey

_____ make wise

_____ give great reward

_____ are righteous

_____ give light

_____ is perfect

_____ are trustworthy

Taking all these characteristics as a whole, what does Psalm 19:7-11 communicate to you about God's law?

_____

_____

_____

_____

_____

Psalm 119 is the longest chapter in the Bible. In the original Hebrew it is an ingenious acrostic poem, meaning that it's divided into twenty-two stanzas, one for each letter of the Hebrew alphabet, and that in each stanza, each of the eight verses begins with the Hebrew letter for that stanza. All of its 176 verses refer to God's law, either as the word *law* or as *statutes, decrees, commandments, word, precepts* or *promises*. We would think the psalm writer would run out of things to say about God's law, but his praise for it—and his longing to obey it—seem endless.

Read the final section, Psalm 119:169-176. In this concluding section, what attitude toward God's law comes through most strongly?

_____

_____

_____

_____

_____

What connection do you see between Psalm 119:160 and Matthew 5:17-18?

_____

_____

_____

_____

_____

---

[1]Martin J. Selman, "Law," in *Dictionary of the Old Testament: Pentateuch,* ed. T. Desmond Alexander and David W. Baker (Downers Grove, IL: InterVarsity Press, 2003), p. 498.
[2]Ibid., p. 501.

PART 3. REFLECT

As Enduring as the Universe

This part of Jesus' sermon divides itself into two parts: first Christ and the law (vv. 17-18) and secondly the Christian and the law (vv. 19-20).

Jesus begins by telling his hearers not for one moment to imagine that he had come to abolish the Law and the Prophets. The way in which Jesus phrases this negative statement suggests that some had indeed been thinking the very thought which he now contradicts. Although his public ministry had so recently begun, already his contemporaries were deeply disturbed by his supposed attitude to the Old Testament.

Certainly from the very beginning of Jesus' ministry, people had been struck by his authority. "What is this?" they asked. "A new teaching—and with authority! He even gives orders to impure spirits and they obey him" (Mark 1:27). It was natural therefore that many were asking what the relation was between *his* authority and the authority of the law of Moses.

People are still asking today, though in different ways, about the relation between Jesus and Moses, the New Testament and the Old.

Jesus said that he came neither to *abolish* the Law and the Prophets, setting them aside or abrogating them, nor even just to endorse them in a dead and literalistic way, but to *fulfill* them. The verb translated "to fulfill" means literally *to fill*. In order to grasp the far-reaching implications of this, we need to recall that the Old Testament contains various kinds of teaching. The relation of Jesus Christ to these differs, but the word *fulfillment* covers them all.

First, the Old Testament contains *doctrinal teaching*. *Torah,* usually translated "law," really means "revealed instruction." All the great biblical doctrines are in the Old Testament. Yet it was only a partial revelation. Jesus fulfilled it all in the sense of bringing it to completion by his person, his teaching and his work.

Second, the Old Testament contains *predictive prophecy*. Much of it looks forward to the days of the Messiah, and either foretells him in word or foreshadows him in type. Yet this was only anticipation. Jesus fulfilled it all in the sense that what was predicted came to pass in him. Again and again he claimed that the Scriptures bore witness to him, and Matthew emphasizes this more than any other Gospel writer by his repeated formula "All this took place to fulfill what the Lord had said through the prophet" (Matthew 1:22). The climax was his death on the cross in which the whole ceremonial system of the Old Testament, both priesthood and sacrifice, found its perfect fulfillment.

Third, the Old Testament contains *ethical principles* or the moral law of God. Yet they were often misunderstood and even more often disobeyed. Jesus fulfilled them in the first instance by obeying them, for he was "born under the law" (Galatians 4:4) and was determined "to fulfill all righteousness" (Matthew 3:15). He does more than obey the commandments himself; he explains what obedience will involve for his disciples. He rejects the superficial interpretation of the law given by the scribes; he himself supplies the true interpretation.

Thus, the attitude of Jesus to the Old Testament was not one of destruction and of discontinuity, but rather of a constructive, organic continuity. Having stated, then, that his purpose in coming was to fulfill the law, Jesus went on to give the cause and the consequence of this. The cause is the permanence of the law until it is fulfilled (v. 18), and the consequence is the obedience to the law which the citizens of God's kingdom must give (vv. 19-20).

This is what Jesus has to say about the law he has come to fulfill: "Truly I tell you, until heaven and earth disappear, not the smallest letter [or "iota," which is Greek for *yod,* the smallest letter of the Hebrew alphabet, almost as small as a comma], not the least stroke of a pen [*keraia*, a horn, referring probably to one of the tiny hooks or projections which distinguish some Hebrew letters from others], will by any means disappear from the Law until everything is accomplished" (v. 18). None of it will pass away or be discarded, Jesus says, not a single letter or part of a letter, until it has all been fulfilled. And this fulfillment will not be complete until heaven and earth themselves pass away. Then the written words of God's law will be needed no longer, for all things in them will have been fulfilled. Thus the law is as enduring as the universe. The final fulfillment of the one and the new birth of the other will coincide. Both will "disappear" together. Jesus could not have stated more clearly than this his own view of Old Testament Scripture.

The word "therefore" in verse 19 introduces the deduction which Jesus now draws for his disciples from the enduring validity of the law and his own attitude with respect to it. It reveals a vital connection between the law of God and the kingdom of God. Because he has come not to abolish but to fulfill, and because not an iota or dot will pass from the law until all has been fulfilled, *therefore* greatness in the kingdom of God will be measured by conformity to it. Nor is personal obedience enough; Christian disciples must also teach to others the permanently binding nature of the law's commandments.

Jesus goes further still. Not only is greatness in the kingdom assessed by a righteousness which conforms to the law, but entry into the kingdom is impossible without a conformity better (*much better;* the Greek expression is very emphatic) than that of the scribes and Pharisees, for God's kingdom is a kingdom of righteousness.

But does this not teach a doctrine of salvation by good works and so contradict the first Beatitude which says the kingdom belongs to the poor in spirit who have nothing, not even righteousness, to plead?

Our Lord's statement must certainly have astonished the first hearers as it astonishes us today. But the answer to these questions is not far to seek. Christian righteousness far surpasses Pharisaic righteousness in kind rather than in degree. It is not that Christians succeed in keeping 240 commandments when the best Pharisees may have scored only 230. No; Christian righteousness is greater than Pharisaic righteousness because it is deeper, being a righteousness of the heart. The righteousness which is pleasing to God is an inward righteousness of mind and motive. For "the LORD looks at the heart" (1 Samuel 16:7).

It was a new heart-righteousness which the prophets foresaw as one of the blessings of the Messianic age. "I will put my law in their minds and write it on their hearts," God promised through Jeremiah (Jeremiah 31:33). How would he do it? He told Ezekiel, "I will put my Spirit in you and move you to follow my decrees and be careful to keep my laws" (Ezekiel 36:27).

Thus God's two promises to put his law within us and to put his Spirit within us coincide. We must not imagine that when we have the Spirit we can dispense with the law, for what the Spirit does in our hearts is precisely to write God's law there. This deep obedience is a righteousness of the heart and is possible only in those whom the Holy Spirit has regenerated and now indwells. This is why entry into God's kingdom is impossible without a righteousness greater than that of the Pharisees. It is because such a righteousness is evidence of the new birth, and no one enters the kingdom without being born again.

What's the main idea in this section?

What is one thing you can act on based on this reading?

PART 4. DISCUSS
Putting It All Together

OPEN

If the Old Testament did not exist, what would be missing in your knowledge of God?

READ MATTHEW 5:17-20.

So far Jesus has spoken of the character of Christians. He has also emphasized the influence we will have in the world if we exhibit this character and if our character bears fruit in "good deeds." In Matthew 5:17-20 he proceeds to further define this character and these good deeds in terms of righteousness. This passage is of great importance not only for its definition of Christian righteousness but also for the light it throws on the relation between the New Testament and the Old Testament, between the gospel and the law.

1. From your reading in "Connect: Scripture to Scripture," how do we know that God had communicated his will to people even before the giving of the Ten Commandments?

2. Why did the rediscovery of the law in King Josiah's time lead to such a spiritual reawakening?

3. What is the significance of God's law being permanent?

4. From the reflection, what are the ways in which Jesus fulfills the law?

5. What is the contrast between a Christian's righteousness and the righteousness of the Pharisees and teachers of the law of Jesus' day?

6. In your Christian experience, what changes have you gone through in how you regard the Old Testament law?

7. How has this lesson challenged your view of the importance of the law for a Christian?

8. Christians often regard *law* as stifling and *gospel* as liberating. How could God's law be as delightful as it is portrayed in Psalm 19?

9. In the reflection you read, "We must not imagine that when we have the Spirit we can dispense with the law, for what the Spirit does in our hearts is precisely to write God's law there." When have you faced a decision and found it easier than you expected to decide because you discovered that God's law was already written in your heart?

10. Based on what Jesus says in this passage, does your righteousness surpass that of the Pharisees and teachers of the law (v. 20)? Why do you answer as you do?

11. What aspects of God's law are most difficult for you to obey, and why?

Take time to pray that God's law will be written even more deeply on your hearts.

WHAT'S WRONG WITH PRIVATE SINS?

Matthew 5:21-30

WHERE WE'RE GOING

The scribes and Pharisees calculated that the law contained 248 commandments and 365 prohibitions. But they were better at arithmetic than obedience. So they tried to make the law's demands less demanding and the law's permissions more permissive. Throughout the Sermon on the Mount, Jesus seeks to reverse this tendency. He came to deepen, not destroy, the law's demands. In this passage he explains the true meaning of the sixth and seventh commandments, the prohibitions against murder and adultery.

> Part 1. Investigate: Matthew 5:21-30 (On Your Own)
>
> Part 2. Connect: Scripture to Scripture (On Your Own)
>
> Part 3. Reflect: A Christian's Righteousness: *Avoiding Anger and Lust* (On Your Own)
>
> Part 4. Discuss: Putting It All Together (With a Group)

A PRAYER TO PRAY

Here's a prayer you can use as you begin your study:

"You have searched me, LORD, and you know me. You know when I sit and when I rise; you perceive my thoughts from afar" (Psalm 139:1-2). Sovereign Lord, no thought or attitude or intention of our hearts is hidden from you. We confess that our thoughts are often lustful or resentful. Help us to stop justifying ourselves by thinking "It's not really so bad," and instead to become open and honest before you. Cleanse our hearts and minds by your pure Spirit, so that we will honor you, not only outwardly but in our most secret places. We pray this in the name of Jesus who died to make us pure. Amen.

PART 1. INVESTIGATE
Matthew 5:21-30

Read Matthew 5:21-30.

1. What standard does Jesus use for determining right and wrong?

2. In verses 21-22 Jesus places murder and unrighteous anger in the same category. How are they related?

3. Jesus warns against calling someone *Raca* (an Aramaic word meaning "empty" or "stupid") or "You fool" (v. 22). Why do you think insults such as these constitute murder in God's sight?

4. What has caused you to lose your temper with people?

5. What do verses 23-26 teach us about broken relationships?

6. Why is Jesus concerned that reconciliation and apologies be made quickly?

5:21-22. *The insult of calling someone "Raca" is about the same as the one that follows it, "You fool!" The punishments are also roughly equal: the (day of God's) judgment, the heavenly Sanhedrin or supreme court, and hell. (Jewish literature described God's heavenly tribunal as a supreme court, or sanhedrin, parallel to the earthly one.) "The hell of fire" is literally "the Gehenna of fire," which refers to the standard Jewish concept of Gehinnom, the opposite of paradise; in Gehinnom the wicked would be burned up (according to some Jewish teachers) or eternally tortured (according to other Jewish teachers).*

5:23-24. *Judaism stressed reconciliation between individuals; God would not accept an outward offering if one had oppressed or mistreated one's neighbor and did not make it right. In the Old Testament God accepted only sacrifices offered with a pure heart toward him and one's neighbor (Gen 4:4-7; Prov 15:8; Is 1:10-15; Jer 6:20; Amos 5:21-24).*

5:25-26. *Again Jesus returns to the image of the heavenly court. Here he may use the custom of debt imprisonment as another image in*

*the parable; this was a
non-Jewish custom, but
Jewish hearers would have
known about it among the
Gentiles. No mercy would be
shown: the amount of
money to be repaid ex-
tended to the last (literally)
quadrans, almost the least
valuable Roman coin, the
equivalent of only a few
minutes' wages.*

5:27-28. *Other Jewish
teachers also looked down
on lust; some even went as
far as Jesus in regarding it
as adultery. The issue is thus
not the doctrine of Jesus'
hearers but their heart. The
Greek word here is the same
as in the opening line of the
tenth commandment in the
Septuagint (the Greek
version of the Old Testa-
ment): "You shall not desire
your neighbor's wife" (Ex
20:17).*

5:29-30. *Corporal punishment (cutting off append-
ages, e.g., Ex 21:24-25) is
easier to bear than capital
punishment, the decree of
eternal death pronounced by
the heavenly court. Some
Jewish thinkers believed that
one would be resurrected in
exactly the form in which
one had died (e.g., with
limbs missing, as in the case
of many martyrs) before
being made whole, and
Jesus employs this image.*

7. When have you either initiated forgiveness or had someone initiate it with you? What was the outcome?

8. What, according to Jesus, is the full meaning of the seventh commandment: "Do not commit adultery" (vv. 27-28)?

9. Lust has been compared to "a cannibal committing suicide by nibbling on himself."[1] How have you seen lust hurt yourself and others?

10. Some Christians have taken verses 29-30 literally and have mutilated their bodies. How do you think Jesus intends us to understand his warnings? In what situations might you need to "gouge out an eye" or "cut off a hand"?

Ask God to help you rid your life of anything that causes you to sin. Pray that you will be able to obey him in your attitudes as well as your actions.

---

[1]Calvin Miller, "A Requiem for Love," *Christianity Today* 34, no. 2 (1990).

PART 2. CONNECT
Scripture to Scripture

ALMOST FROM THE FIRST PAGE

We don't get very far into the Bible before we are faced with the first murder. The story of Cain killing Abel, from untold years ago, still shocks us with its pathos and its bluntness. Clearly murder is a terrible crime, not only against another human being, but against God the Creator.

Read Genesis 4:1-16. In what verses do you find the following?

The reason for Cain's anger against Abel: _____

God's caution to Cain: _____

Evidence of Cain's premeditation: _____

God's empathy with Abel the victim: _____

Evidence of God's mercy toward Cain: _____

From the beginning of human history, murder was an abomination to God. God made the reason why clear to Noah and his family after the flood.

Read Genesis 9:4-6. In your own words, explain why murder was—and is—so offensive to God.

_____

_____

_____

_____

_____

So it was not a new thing when the sixth commandment of the ten given on Mount Sinai stated "You shall not murder" (Exodus 20:13). There were, however, some clarifications and elaborations. Read the extension of the commandment in Exodus 21:12-14. What difference does it make whether the killer has the premeditated intention to kill the victim?

_____

_____

_____

_____

_____

If the life of the victim was important to God, so was the life of the person who killed by accident and therefore did not deserve to be executed. Read Numbers 35:9-34, which explains the place of safety which the Lord said he would designate in Exodus 21:13. What is the purpose of the six towns of refuge (vv. 9-15)?

_____

_____

_____

_____

_____

Verses 16-25 mention several possible circumstances of one person causing the death of another. Why would striking with an iron object, a stone or a wooden object (vv. 16-18) be evidence of a deliberate intention to kill?

_____

_____

_____

_____

_____

In the cases of murder by shoving, throwing something or hitting with the fist (vv. 20-21), what additional condition is added which points out the killer's intention?

_____

_____

_____

_____

_____

Read Numbers 35:22-25. How do these possible circumstances differ from the circumstances of verses 16-21?

_____

_____

_____

_____

_____

_____

Murder and manslaughter look alike. In both cases one person causes the death of another. In both cases we can identify killer and victim. In God's eyes, however, and therefore in the eyes of the law, externals are not the issue. It is the killer's intention, the killer's heart, which determines whether the killer should receive the ultimate penalty or should be allowed to escape to a town of refuge.

As scholar Dónal P. O'Mathúna explains, "Murder's distinguishing feature is the perpetrator's intention, captured by the term *sediyya* (Num 35:20, 22; cf. Ex. 21:13). This word can be translated as 'lying in wait,' referring to an action, or as 'hatred' or 'enmity,' referring to the actor's state of mind (Ex 21:12-14). The root of the word refers to hunting and is compatible with either the idea of lying in wait intending to do destruction or of having malicious intent. In contrast, manslaughter is characterized as without design, inadvertent, unwitting or an act of God. So long as the victim was not viewed as an enemy and not approached with malicious intent to cause injury, the death was judged as manslaughter, not murder, and was not punished by death (Num 35:22-24; Deut 19:11-13)."[1]

How would you contrast the heart of a deliberate murderer with the heart of an accidental killer?

_____

_____

_____

_____

_____

Because conviction of murder meant execution, the verdict was not reached lightly. Fill in the missing words in Numbers 35:30.

"Anyone who kills a person is to be put to death as a murderer _____

_____. But no one is to be put to death _____."

What would these rules and specifications related to murder and manslaughter have communicated to the Israelites about God?

_____

_____

_____

_____

LOVE YOUR NEIGHBOR
Read Leviticus 19:16-18. How would obedience to these laws prevent the Israelites from coming anywhere close to deliberately murdering one another?

_____

_____

_____

_____

_____

Write out verse 18 word for word:

_____

_____

_____

_____

_____

O'Mathúna adds, "The value of each person as an image of God is not restricted to external action and restraint of violence. Foreshadowing the message of Jesus, the Pentateuch calls on the people of God not to hate their fellow citizens in their hearts but to love their neighbors as themselves (Lev 19:16-18)."[2]

ADULTERY FORBIDDEN

Like murder, adultery was and is offensive to God the Creator, who made human beings in his own image.

As we saw in session three, part two, even before the Ten Commandments were given, Joseph knew that succumbing to the advances of Potiphar's wife would be sinning against God (Genesis 39:6-10).

Read Deuteronomy 22:22-27. Complete the following statements:

For both parties, the penalty for adultery was _____.

The severity of the penalty startles us today. The reason given for such a harsh penalty is that

_____.

We must take into account that the law did not automatically dispense such harsh justice in all seemingly adulterous circumstances. Immediately after the stark judgment of verse 22, the law becomes flexible to accommodate specific situations. There was no penalty for the woman if she had been forced by the man. God is always concerned with the will of the person, regardless of outward appearances, and an unwilling partner could not justly be punished.

How were judges to differentiate whether the woman was a willing person?

_____

_____

_____

_____

_____

Consider why a distinction was made for whether the occurrence happened in the country or in the town. If it took place in a town and the evidence was that the woman did not cry out for help, the assumption was that _____.

If it took place in the countryside, the woman received mercy because _____

_____.

God's law is severe toward anyone who *willingly* has sexual relations with anyone besides the person's marital partner. The provision against adultery is not some priggish rule by a divine kill-joy; it is God's protective measure to guard sexual purity within and outside of marriage.

Read Proverbs 6:20-35, in which a wise father warns his son against committing adultery. The father says that the man who commits adultery "destroys himself" (v. 32). Write the numbers of verses in the passage that identify the ways that the man can harm or endanger himself.

verse numbers: _____

As is the case with instructions related to murder, we see evidence in the Old Testament that the Israelites knew adultery is both an internal and external act, as Jesus explains in the Sermon on the Mount. Job is one source of the evidence for this when he defends his righteousness to God in an attempt to make sense of his physical and mental suffering. Read Job 31:1-12, part of Job's claim of righteous living. What does Job claim specifically about his sexual ethics?

_____

_____

_____

How does Job claim innocence not only externally but inwardly?

_____

_____

_____

Scholar Walter Kaiser explains that Job's covenant with his eyes (Job 31:1) "was no manifestation of moral heroism on his part, but a decision that was in accord with the Word of God. In fact, according to Job 31:4, Job realized that God saw everything; all of a person's ways were open before the Lord. . . . On these points there is very little difference between the moral expectations of the New Testament and those of the Old. The teaching of our Lord through Job's book and the teaching of Jesus in the Sermon on the Mount are harmonious."[3]

SPIRITUAL ADULTERY

The Lord commanded the Israelites specifically not to commit adultery or lust after another man's wife in the seventh and tenth commands of the Ten Commandments, but he also repeatedly warned them against another kind of adultery, one that breaks the first two commandments and thus the rest of the law as well. Read the Lord's words to Moses in Deuteronomy 31:14-18, given shortly before Moses died.

What is the imagery of verse 16?

_____

_____

_____

_____

_____

Why is this an apt image for the worship of false gods?

_____

_____

_____

_____

_____

Read Judges 2:6-17. How quickly were the Lord's words to Moses fulfilled?

_____

_____

_____

_____

_____

The God who reigns in heaven was not ashamed to call himself Israel's husband and to refer to his relationship with Israel as a covenant of marriage. This covenant, however, was broken by Israel's idolatry, which the prophets consistently equate with spiritual adultery.

The book of Hosea offers the most dramatic example of idolatry as spiritual adultery against God. Hosea was called on to enact physically what Israel was doing spiritually.

Read Hosea 1:1–2:23. Draw lines to match up the following verse numbers with their content.

God calls on Israel to put away her unfaithfulness   Hosea 1:2-3

God promises to punish Israel for idolatry   Hosea 1:4-9

Children are born to Hosea's wife   Hosea 2:2

Hosea marries Gomer   Hosea 2:3-13

God promises to take Israel back and remove her idolatry   Hosea 2:14-23

In Hosea we see that Israel's spiritual adultery is not the end of the story. We see the same compassion on the part of the Lord later, in the time of King Josiah, as spoken through the prophet Jeremiah. Read Jeremiah 3:6-18 and identify all the references to *adultery* and *unfaithfulness* in the passage:

Verse numbers: _____

Despite such persistent idolatry on the part of his people, the Lord pointed the prophet forward to a time when he would change the people's hearts, when the Ark of the Covenant, that holiest of Israel's objects, "will never enter their minds or be remembered; it will not be missed, nor will another one be made" (v. 16). This can only be pointing toward the time of the Messiah; the Ark of the Covenant and the temple which contained it became obsolete once Jesus, the Messiah, made the final, perfect sacrifice for sin.

During the Babylonian exile, the prophet Ezekiel was given an extended—and in some places quite graphic—word-picture of spiritual adultery. Read Ezekiel 16.

In verses 30-34, how is this adulterous wife even worse than a prostitute?

_____

_____

_____

_____

_____

How do verses 59-63 resemble the assurances of Jeremiah 3:14-18 and Hosea 2:14-23?

_____

_____

_____

_____

_____

GOD'S LAWS, GOD'S HEART

The spiritualizing of idolatry-as-adultery did not negate the plainer meaning of the seventh commandment. The promised Messiah himself made that clear in his Sermon on the Mount when he said that the law will remain as long as heaven and earth remain. God's eternal laws reveal God's eternal love for humanity and the value he places on each human life. God wants only the best for each person, and the best for each of us is revealed in the law of God.

---

[1]Dónal P. O'Mathúna, "Bodily Injuries, Murder, Manslaughter," in *Dictionary of the Old Testament: Pentateuch*, ed. T. Desmond Alexander and David W. Baker (Downers Grove, IL: InterVarsity Press, 2003), p. 91.
[2]Ibid.
[3]Walter Kaiser Jr., Peter H. Davids, F. F. Bruce and Manfred Brauch, *Hard Sayings of the Bible* (Downers Grove, IL: InterVarsity Press, 1996), p. 261.

PART 3. REFLECT
A Christian's Righteousness
AVOIDING ANGER AND LUST

In Matthew 5:21-48 we find six parallel paragraphs which illustrate the principle of the perpetuity of the moral law, of Jesus' coming to fulfill it and of his disciples' responsibility to obey it more completely than the scribes and the Pharisees were doing. Each paragraph contains a contrast or antithesis introduced by the same formula (with minor variations): "You have heard that it was said . . . But I tell you . . ."

What is this antithesis? With whom is Jesus contrasting himself? Many commentators have maintained that Jesus is setting himself against Moses, as if to say "You know what the Old Testament taught, but I teach something quite different." Popular as this interpretation is, I do not hesitate to say that it is untenable. What Jesus is contradicting is not the law itself, but certain perversions of the law of which the scribes and Pharisees were guilty. Four arguments will be sufficient to prove that this is so.

First, there is the substance of the antitheses themselves. At first sight in each instance what Jesus quotes appears to come from the Mosaic law. All six examples either consist of or include some echo of it; but when we come to the sixth and last antithesis, we see that something is amiss. "You have heard that it was said, 'Love your neighbor and hate your enemy'" (Matthew 5:43). The first half of the sentence is a truncated version of Leviticus 19:18, but the second half is not in the law at all. So here was a contemporary addition to the law, which was intended to interpret it but in fact distorted it. When we look at the other five antitheses, it becomes plain that a similar distortion is implied. It is these distortions of the law which Jesus rejected, not the law itself.

Second, there is the introductory formula, "You have heard that it was said" or "It has been said." The words "it was said" represent the single Greek verb *errethē*. Now this was not the word Jesus used in quoting Scripture. When he introduced a biblical quotation, he used *gegraptai*, "It stands written," not *errethē*, "It was said." So in the six antitheses, Jesus was contradicting not Scripture but tradition, not God's word which they had "read" but the oral instruction which they had "heard."

Third, there is the immediate context. We have already seen that in verses 17-20, Jesus affirmed in a quite unequivocal way what his own attitude to the law was and what his disciples' ought to be. This was fulfillment in his case and obedience in theirs. Not a dot or iota would pass away; all must be fulfilled. Not one of the least commandments might be disregarded; all must be obeyed. Are we now seriously to suppose that Jesus contradicted himself, that he proceeded at once in his teaching to do what he had just categorically said he had not come to do and they must not do? If in the antitheses Jesus was contradicting Moses, he was thereby contradicting himself.

Fourth, there is Christ's known attitude to the Old Testament. Matthew 4:1-11 gives an account of his temptations during forty grueling days in the Judean desert. Each subtle enticement of the devil was countered by an appropriate quotation from Old Testament Scripture. Jesus had no need to debate or argue with the devil. Each issue was settled from the start by a simple appeal to what stood written (*gegraptai*). This reverent submission of the incarnate Word to the written word continued throughout his life, not only in his personal behavior but also in his mission. So his declaration in Matthew 5:17 that he had come not to abolish but to fulfill the Law and the Prophets is wholly consistent with his attitude to Scripture elsewhere.

From these four factors it is evident that the antitheses do not set in opposition to each other Christ and Moses, the New Testament and the Old Testament, the gospel and the law, but rather Christ's true interpretation of the law and the scribal misinterpretations, and therefore Christian righteousness and Pharisaic righteousness.

What the scribes and Pharisees were doing, in order to make obedience more readily attainable, was to restrict the commandments and extend the permissions of the law. They made the law's demands less demanding and the law's permissions more permissive. What Jesus did was to reverse both tendencies. He insisted instead that the full implications of God's commandments must be accepted without imposing any artificial limits, whereas the limits which God had set to his permissions must also be accepted and not arbitrarily increased.

The first two illustrations which Jesus gave of his theme relate to the sixth and seventh of the Ten Commandments, the prohibitions against murder and adultery.

The commandment "You shall not murder" (Exodus 20:13) is not a prohibition against taking human life in any and every circumstance, but in particular against homicide. This is clear from the fact that the same Mosaic law, which forbids killing in the Decalogue, elsewhere enjoins it both in the form of capital punishment and in the wars designed to exterminate the corrupt pagan tribes which inhabited the Promised Land. Both war and the death penalty are vexed questions which have always perplexed sensitive Christian consciences. And there have always been Christians on both sides of both fences. What needs always to be asserted by Christians in these debates is that, if the concept of the "just war" is tenable and if the retention of the

death penalty is justifiable, the reason is not because human life is ever cheap and readily disposable but the very opposite, namely, that it is precious as the life of creatures made in God's image. I mention these things now, not because the complex issues involved in war and the death penalty can be treated here, but to argue that they cannot be solved by a simplistic appeal to the commandment "You shall not kill."

The scribes and the Pharisees were evidently seeking to restrict the application of the sixth commandment to the deed of murder alone. If they refrained from spilling human blood in homicide, they considered that they had kept the commandment. This apparently is what the rabbis taught the people. But Jesus disagreed with them. The true application of the prohibition was much wider, he maintained. It included thoughts and words as well as deeds, anger and insult as well as murder. Not all anger is evil, as is evident from the wrath of God, which is always holy and pure; and even fallen human beings may sometimes feel righteous anger. The reference of Jesus is to unrighteous anger, the anger of pride, vanity, hatred, malice and revenge.

Now, angry thoughts and insulting words may never lead to the ultimate act of murder. Yet they are tantamount to murder in God's sight. As John was later to write, "Anyone who hates a brother or sister is a murderer" (1 John 3:15). Anger and insult are ugly symptoms of a desire to get rid of somebody who stands in our way. Our thoughts, looks and words all indicate that, as we sometimes dare to say, we wish the person were dead. Such an evil wish is a breach of the sixth commandment.

"Therefore," Jesus continued (Matthew 5:23), and proceeded to give a practical application of the principles he had just enunciated. If anger and insult are so serious and so dangerous, then we must avoid them like the plague and take action as speedily as possible. He offered two illustrations. One is taken from worship, the other from the law court. One concerns a "brother or sister," the other an "adversary" (vv. 23, 25). But in both cases the basic situation is the same (somebody has a grievance against us) and the basic lesson is the same (the necessity of immediate, urgent action). In the very act of worship, if we remember the grievance, we are to break off our worship and go and put it right. In the very act of going to court, on our way there, we are to settle our debt.

Yet how seldom do we heed Christ's call for immediacy of action! We must never allow an estrangement to remain, still less to grow. We must not delay to put it right. *Immediately*, as soon as we are conscious of a broken relationship, we must take the initiative to mend it, to apologize for the grievance we have caused, to pay the debt we have left unpaid, to make amends.

Jesus now turns from the sixth commandment to the seventh, from the prohibition against murder to the prohibition against adultery. Here again the rabbis were attempting to limit the scope of the commandment "You shall not commit adultery" (Exodus 20:14). Although the sin of desiring another man's wife is included in the tenth commandment against covetousness (Exodus 20:17), they evidently found it more comfortable to ignore this. They gave a conveniently narrow definition of sexual sin and a conveniently broad definition of sexual purity.

But Jesus taught differently. He affirmed that the true meaning of God's command was much wider than a mere prohibition of acts of sexual immorality. We can commit murder with our *words;* we can commit adultery in our *hearts* or minds.

What is especially important to grasp is Jesus' equation of *looking* lustfully and committing adultery in the heart. It is the relation between the eyes and the heart which leads Jesus in the next two verses to give some very practical instruction about how to maintain sexual purity. If to look lustfully is to commit adultery in the heart, in other words if heart-adultery is the result of eye-adultery (the eyes of the heart being stimulated by the eyes of the flesh), then the only way to deal with the problem is at its beginning, which is our eyes.

This teaching of Jesus is still true today. Deeds of shame are preceded by fantasies of shame, and the inflaming of the imagination by the indiscipline of the eyes. Our vivid imagination is a precious gift of God. But all God's gifts need to be used responsibly; they can readily be deranged and abused. I doubt if ever human beings have fallen victim to immorality, who have not first opened the sluice gates of passion through their eyes. Similarly, whenever men and women have learned sexual self-control in deed, it is because they have first learned it in the eyes of both flesh and fantasy.

On the surface it is a startling command to gouge out an offending eye or to cut off an offending hand (Matthew 5:29-30). This was evidently a favorite saying of Jesus, for he quoted it more than once. It recurs later in Matthew 18:8-9, where the foot is added to the eye and the hand, and the reference is a general one to temptations to sin. This is an example of our Lord's use of dramatic figures of speech. What he was advocating was not a literal physical self-maiming, but a ruthless moral self-denial. Not mutilation but mortification is the path of holiness he taught, and mortification—taking up the cross to follow Christ—means to reject sinful practices so resolutely that we die to them or put them to death.

If your eye causes you to sin because temptation comes to you through your eyes (objects or images you see), then gouge out your eyes. That is, don't look! Behave as if you had actually gouged out your eyes and flung them away, and were now blind and so *could* not see the objects or images which previously caused you to sin. Again, if your hand or foot causes you to sin because temptation comes to you through your hands (things you do) or your feet (places you visit), then cut them off. Don't do it! Don't go! Behave as if you had actually cut off your hands and feet, and were now crippled and so *could* not do the things or visit the places which previously caused you to sin.

What is necessary for all those with strong sexual temptations, and indeed for all of us in principle, is discipline in guarding the approaches of sin. The posting of sentries is a commonplace of military tactics. Moral sentry duty is equally indispensable. Are we so foolish as to allow the enemy to overwhelm us, simply because we have posted no sentries to warn us of his approach?

What's the main idea in this section?

What is one thing you can act on based on this reading?

PART 4. DISCUSS
Putting It All Together

OPEN

What advice would you give to someone who is struggling to get along with an irritating individual?

READ MATTHEW 5:21-30.

Jesus' teaching here is based on the principle that eternity is more important than time, and purity than culture, and that any sacrifice is worthwhile in this life if it is necessary to ensure our entry into the next. We have to decide, quite simply, whether to live for this world or the next, whether to follow the crowd or Jesus Christ.

1. In this Scripture passage, what standard does Jesus use for determining right and wrong?

2. From the reading, how had the scribal traditions of oral teaching altered the original intent of the law?

3. How did the law differentiate between murder and accidental killing?

4. What practical instruction do verses 23-26 offer about broken relationships?

5. What difference does it make to remember that other people—whether people we hate or people we look at lustfully—are made in the image of God?

6. Do you feel that the judgments of verse 22 are too harsh or appropriate, and why?

7. When have you been glad that you settled a conflict quickly?

8. Why is lust, even when kept secret, destructive to relationships?

9. Why is adultery such a suitable image for idolatry?

10. In connection with verses 29-30, you read in the reflection the straightforward advice, "Don't look! Don't do it! Don't go!" What aspects of our culture make that advice difficult to put into practice?

11. Temptations to sin typically approach us through the eyes. The reading stated, "The posting of sentries is a commonplace of military tactics. Moral sentry duty is equally indispensable." What are some practical ways you can post sentries against temptation?

Pray for freedom from both unrighteous anger and lust. Thank God for his forgiveness and his faithfulness.

FAITHFULNESS IN MARRIAGE AND SPEECH

Matthew 5:31-37; 19:3-9

WHERE WE'RE GOING

Jesus' third antithesis (about divorce) follows the second (about adultery) as a natural sequence. For in certain circumstances, Jesus now says, remarriage by or to a divorced person is tantamount to adultery. This third antithesis is essentially a call to fidelity in marriage. I confess to a basic reluctance to attempt an exposition of these verses. Yet it is because I am convinced that the teaching of Jesus on this and every subject is good—intrinsically good, good for individuals, good for society—that I take my courage in both hands and write on.

Part 1. Investigate: Matthew 5:31-37; 19:3-9 (On Your Own)

Part 2. Connect: Scripture to Scripture (On Your Own)

Part 3. Reflect: A Christian's Righteousness: *Fidelity in Marriage and Honesty in Speech* (On Your Own)

Part 4. Discuss: Putting It All Together (With a Group)

A PRAYER TO PRAY

Here's a prayer you can use to get started:

God of truth, there is no deceit or falsehood in you. Your word is true and trustworthy. You faithfully keep your promises. You do not flatter us but rather are honest with us about our sin. We ask that our lives would always reflect your faithfulness and your honesty. Help us to honor our commitments, whether with family, in business or in any other sphere of life. Help us to refrain from foolish impulsive promises, and to keep the promises that we make. We pray this in the name of Jesus, who is the way, the truth and the life. Amen.

PART 1. INVESTIGATE
Matthew 5:31-37; 19:3-9

5:31-32. *Some Pharisaic rabbis allowed divorce for almost anything (just as Roman law did); others allowed it only if the wife were unfaithful. Yet the stricter rabbis did not view more lenient divorces as invalid. Jesus thus goes beyond the stricter position: not only does he allow divorce only if one's wife is unfaithful, but he regards divorce for any other reason as invalid, thus making remarriage in those cases adulterous. This seems, however, to be hyperbole (as in 5:29-30), a graphic way of forbidding divorce except when the other partner has already irreparably broken the marriage covenant.*

If Jesus' interpretation of the law was stricter than what the law said at face value, no one would have thought that he was therefore contradicting the law; "building a fence" around the law was a standard Jewish practice that involved making certain that the law's intent was not broken.

19:8. *Jewish teachers of the law recognized a legal category called "concession": something that was permitted only because it was better to regulate sin*

Read Matthew 5:31-37 and 19:3-9.

1. How do Jesus' statements contrast with the questions about divorce that he was asked by the Pharisees?

2. At the time of Christ, a controversy about divorce was being conducted between the rival schools of Rabbi Hillel and Rabbi Shammai. Rabbi Shammai taught that divorce was permitted only in extreme cases. Rabbi Hillel taught that it was permitted for any and every reason. How does this help us to understand the Pharisees' "test" question (19:3)?

3. Jesus points back to Genesis. What do Jesus' words teach us about God's original design for marriage (19:4-6)?

4. How can you prepare for or live out a marriage that meets God's original design?

What difference does God's design make in living as a married couple?

5. The Pharisees refer to Moses' instructions about divorce as a "command" (19:7). What does Jesus' reply teach us about divorce (19:8)?

than to relinquish control over it altogether. Given God's purpose in creation (Gen 2:24), divorce naturally fell into such a category (cf. Mal 2:14-16).

In what ways might divorce reveal the hardness of our hearts?

19:9. *The school of Shammai did not permit divorce except for the wife's unfaithfulness (whether successful or attempted), but they did not consider remarriage afterward adulterous. Jesus is more consistent: if one divorces one's spouse without valid grounds (unfaithfulness or analogous sins; cf. 1 Cor 7:10-13), the marriage is not truly dissolved and subsequent marriage is adulterous. This statement (that all subsequent unions are invalid unless the first marriage was dissolved by infidelity) may be hyperbolic rather than literal, but hyperbole is stated the way it is to make its point forcefully, not to be ignored. Divorce must never be taken lightly.*

6. What similarities and differences are there between 19:9 and 5:31-32?

How do these verses stress the seriousness of divorce?

7. How does Jesus' teaching contrast with today's views that you and your peers have held concerning marriage and divorce?

Because men could divorce women unilaterally but women could demand a divorce only under certain very narrow conditions (and then needed the court's help), Jesus' opposition to this sort of divorce is also a defense of married women.

8. Reread Matthew 5:33-37. How might the issue of oaths and vows be connected to the topic of marriage and divorce?

5:33-37. *People swore by all sorts of things other than God to testify that their word was true. They reasoned that if they broke their oath based on any of these lesser things, at least they were not bringing God's name into disrepute. It eventually became necessary for rabbis to decide which oaths were completely binding. Jesus says that everything by which one could swear is ultimately God's, and demands that people simply be as good as their word. Jesus argues the point in part from Scripture; Isaiah 66:1 declared that heaven is God's throne and earth is his footstool.*

9. The Pharisees had elaborate formulas for oaths, with some being binding and some not (see Matthew 23:16-22). Why is Jesus opposed to oaths?

10. Does this mean, for example, that we should refuse to give evidence under oath in a court of law? Explain.

11. Why should oaths be unnecessary for Jesus' followers?

Ask God to help you resist the pressures to compromise in marriage and in speech.

5:36. *Most people in Jewish Palestine had black or dark hair, unless they were older, in which case their hair was turning white; verse 36 would have been heard as referring to God's control over aging. Jesus' rule here is stricter than the letter of the law but in accord with its spirit (Deut 23:21-23; Eccles 5:5).*

PART 2. CONNECT
Scripture to Scripture

ORIGINAL MARRIAGE

The concept of marriage between a woman and a man comes very early in Scripture. Read Genesis 2:15-25. We know from Genesis 1:31 that God pronounced his whole creation "very good," yet here one thing in Eden is called "not good." What is it?

_____

_____

_____

_____

_____

Fill in the missing parts of Genesis 2:24:

"That is why a man _____ and is _____,

and they _____."

How do you interpret the phrase "That is why" in Genesis 2:24?

_____

_____

_____

_____

_____

God's intentions and design for marriage are clearly laid out from the beginning, evident in Adam and Eve's relationship that God created and ordained. As Bible scholar Gordon Wenham notes, "God created only one Eve for Adam, not several Eves or another Adam, thereby indicating divine disapproval of both polygamy (cf. Lv. 18:18; Dt. 17:17) and homosexual practice (Lv. 18:22; Rom. 1:26-27)."[1] Marriage, by God's design and intentions, is only between one woman and one man; any other arrangement is not biblical marriage.

GOD'S PROVISIONS IN A BROKEN WORLD

God's law nowhere specifies how a marriage is to be performed. Neither does it specify how a divorce might be conducted. Indeed, the concept of divorce first appears in Scripture in regard to situations in which divorce, or marriage with a divorced person, are not allowed.

Read Deuteronomy 22:13-19. Describe the situation which gives rise to the dispute.

_____

_____

_____

_____

Complete this statement:

A husband who falsely accused his wife of unchastity could never divorce her. God's law pro-

hibited divorce in that situation because _____.

Read Deuteronomy 24:1-4.
What does verse 4 specifically prohibit, and why?

_____

_____

_____

_____

Verses 1-3 give a rather sad series of hypothetical conditions. Fill in the conditions in the
blanks. It is not necessary to copy the exact words of Scripture.

First a man _____. Then he finds _____. Then

he writes _____, gives it _____ and sends

_____. Then the woman _____. Then her second husband

_____ and writes _____, gives it _____

and sends _____ or possibly he _____. If all those things happen,

then her first husband _____.

"The point of the law is merely to prevent a return to the first husband after a second marriage
of the divorced woman has ended. (Je. 3:1-5 presupposes this point.) The aim may have been to
make divorce so solemn and final that it would not be entered upon lightly."[2]

Deuteronomy 24:1 allows a man to divorce his wife if she "becomes displeasing to him because
he finds something indecent about her." With such grave consequences at stake, we naturally ask
what constitutes "something indecent," but the answer is not crystal clear. Hebrew Scripture literally says "nakedness of a thing." "The precise meaning of 'nakedness of a thing' is disputed. Many
interpreters believe that this term excludes adultery, since adultery was a grounds for execution,
not divorce. . . . However, the matter is complicated. The word 'nakedness' ('erwā) is used fre-
quently in an idiom for sexual intercourse, . . . so sexual connotations seem likely."[3]

Scholar David Instone-Brewer has done extensive research into what the Bible says about divorce and remarriage. He holds that "the Old Testament recognizes four grounds for divorce. The first three are neglecting to provide food, clothing and conjugal love (by either husband or wife), and the fourth is committing adultery. . . . Abusive situations were covered by these laws, because physical abuse and emotional abuse are extreme forms of neglecting material support and physical affection." Instone-Brewer points to Exodus 21:7-11, which "allows the victim of abuse or neglect to be freed from the marriage." In a culture where polygamy was practiced, "the point of this law was to ensure that the first wife was treated fairly. It says that the husband would not be permitted to withhold food, clothing or conjugal love from her. If he did neglect any of these, she would be able to go free—that is, she could get divorced."

By the time of Christ, rabbinic interpretation of the law had stretched several points, and a new "Any Cause" divorce had come into practice, invented by Rabbi Hillel. It was based on a loose interpretation of Deuteronomy 24:1. Disciples of another rabbi, Rabbi Shammai, "wanted people to restrict themselves to divorces based on the Old Testament grounds—unfaithfulness in Deuteronomy 24:1 and neglect of food, clothing or conjugal love in Exodus 21:10-11. But the common people preferred Hillel's interpretation, which added the 'Any Cause' divorce."

Instone-Brewer holds that when the Pharisees questioned Jesus about divorce in Matthew 19:3, they were referring *only* to Deuteronomy 24:1, and that Jesus answered them *only* in regard to Deuteronomy 24:1, limiting that passage of Scripture to adultery and rejecting the "Any Cause" grounds for divorce.[4]

The last book in the Old Testament is the book of the prophet Malachi, who was active in Judah after the return from Babylon. The temple of the Lord had been rebuilt, but Malachi admonished the people for offering defiled and inadequate sacrifices there. At the conclusion of his prophecy he looked forward to the coming of Elijah the prophet to prepare the people for the Lord's coming. The covenant of marriage finds a place in these great themes.

Read Malachi 2:13-16.

What attitude were the people showing in their worship?

_____

_____

_____

_____

_____

How did the Lord explain the cause of the situation?

_____

_____

_____

_____

_____

The 2011 New International Version translates Malachi 2:16 as

> "The man who hates and divorces his wife," says the LORD, the God of Israel, "does violence to the one he should protect," says the LORD Almighty.

A footnote for that verse provides an alternate translation:

> "I hate divorce," says the LORD, the God of Israel, "because the man who divorces his wife covers his garment with violence," says the LORD Almighty.

How do both possible translations agree on God's attitude toward divorce?

_____

_____

_____

_____

_____

The *Dictionary of Biblical Imagery* highlights that "the motif of a permanent bond is another dimension of marriage in the Bible. The ideal is that marriage is for life. Such permanence does not force something foreign onto romantic passion but is an ideal to which romantic love itself propels people when they are in love."[5] The Old Testament picture of marriage is of something serious, joyful, blessed by God and not lightly broken.

At the very least, it is only when a person has understood and accepted God's view of marriage and God's call to reconciliation that a possible context has been created within which one may regretfully go on to talk about divorce.

SPEAKING OF VOWS . . .

The third commandment is, "You shall not misuse the name of the LORD your God, for the LORD will not hold anyone guiltless who misuses his name" (Exodus 20:7). John Walton, Victor Matthews and Mark Chavalas clarify that "this commandment does not refer to blasphemy or foul language. Rather it is intended to prevent the exploitation of the name of Yahweh for magical purposes or hexing. It also continues the concerns of the second commandment in that someone's name was believed to be intimately connected to that person's being and essence. The giving of one's name was an act of favor, trust and, in human terms, vulnerability. Israel was not to attempt to use Yahweh's name in magical ways to manipulate him. The commandment was also intended to insure that the use of Yahweh's name in oaths, vows and treaties was taken seriously."[6]

In other words, a person who swore an oath by the name of the Lord was calling on the Lord to witness the vow and to see to it that the vow was kept. "If I don't keep this vow," the person was saying, "may God take vengeance on me." They were serious words and needed to be taken seriously.

Read Leviticus 19:12. What is forbidden, and why?

_____

_____

_____

_____

_____

_____

Read Isaiah 48:1-2. How was Israel misusing the name of the Lord?

_____

_____

_____

_____

_____

Words come easily. It costs nothing to say "As God is my witness, I will do this," and people did—and still do—make such statements flippantly. The Old Testament is clear that God holds people to such vows.

Read Numbers 30:1-2 and Deuteronomy 23:21-23. Respond to the following statements as true or false:

_____ It is better to make a vow than not to make one because at least the person has the right intention.

_____ Keeping part of a vow is as good as keeping the entire vow because God sees the heart.

_____ It is better to avoid making a vow than to make one and not fulfill it.

_____ The time frame of keeping a vow does not matter; what matters is keeping it.

_____ Neglecting a vow is an oversight rather than a sin.

_____ Promptness in keeping a vow shows obedience to the Lord.

A VOW FULFILLED

An example of a vow fulfilled is found in Joshua 2. In advance of invading Canaan, Joshua sent two spies into Jericho. Read Joshua 2:1-14.

Paraphrase the conversation between Rahab and the spies in Joshua 2:12-14:

Rahab: "_____

_____."

The spies: "_____

_____."

Read Joshua 6:22-25. How did Joshua keep the vow which the spies had made?

_____

_____

_____

_____

_____

HASTY VOWS

Proverbs 20:25 says "It is a trap to dedicate something rashly and only later to consider one's vows." Why would a hasty vow be a "trap"?

_____

_____

_____

_____

_____

Read Ecclesiastes 5:1-7. Choose the best completion for each statement:

Don't be too quick to make vows in the house of God because

____ a. it is a sacred space.

____ b. it is better to listen than to speak.

____ c. someone might overhear you and repeat what you say.

____ d. certain language is not proper there.

The "sacrifice of fools" is

____ a. unclean animals.

____ b. a sacrifice brought at the wrong time.

____ c. forgetting to make vows before the Lord.

____ d. hasty vows before the Lord.

Rather than make a vow and not fulfill it, do not vow at all, because

____ a. God takes your vows seriously.

____ b. then you won't forget.

____ c. the temple messenger might misunderstand you.

____ d. you might dream that you made a vow.

Explain how you would interpret the meaning of Ecclesiastes 5:2:

> God is in heaven
>> and you are on earth,
>> so let your words be few.

_____

_____

_____

_____

_____

Biblical scholar Christopher J. H. Wright notes, "OT law nowhere commands the making of vows or the dedication of people or things to God (apart from the regular tithe and firstfruits and consecration of the firstborn sons). Special vows were entirely voluntary. What the law did insist on, however, was that people should not make rash vows or commitments and then fail to keep them. God should not be trifled with, and promises made to him must be treated as seriously as promises made to any human person."[7]

In view of the seriousness of oaths and the danger of misusing God's name, Jesus' words "Do not swear at all" make perfect sense as the wisest and safest course to take.

[1]Gordon J. Wenham, "Genesis," in *New Bible Commentary*, ed. G. J. Wenham, J. A. Motyer, D. A. Carson and R. T. France, 21st century ed. (Downers Grove, IL: InterVarsity Press, 1994), p. 62.

[2]Gordon McConville, "Deuteronomy," in *New Bible Commentary*, ed. G. J. Wenham, J. A. Motyer, D. A. Carson and R. T. France, 21st century ed. (Downers Grove, IL: InterVarsity Press, 1994), p. 220.

[3]Joe M. Sprinkle, "Sexuality, Sexual Ethics," *Dictionary of the Old Testament: Pentateuch*, ed. T. Desmond Alexander and David W. Baker (Downers Grove, IL: InterVarsity Press, 2003), p. 744.

[4]David Instone-Brewer, *Divorce and Remarriage in the Church* (Downers Grove, IL: InterVarsity Press, 2003), pp. 35, 37, 55, 57, 96-97.

[5]Leland Ryken, James C. Wilhoit and Tremper Longman, eds., "Marriage," in *Dictionary of Biblical Imagery* (Downers Grove, IL: InterVarsity Press, 1998), p. 538.

[6]John H. Walton, Victor H. Matthews and Mark W. Chavalas, *The IVP Bible Background Commentary: Old Testament* (Downers Grove, IL: InterVarsity Press, 2000), p. 95.

[7]Christopher J. H. Wright, "Leviticus," in *New Bible Commentary*, ed. G. J. Wenham, J. A. Motyer, D. A. Carson and R. T. France, 21st century ed. (Downers Grove, IL: InterVarsity Press, 1994), pp. 155-56.

PART 3. REFLECT
A Christian's Righteousness
FIDELITY IN MARRIAGE AND HONESTY IN SPEECH

Matthew 5:31-32 can hardly be thought to represent the sum total of our Lord's instruction on the mountain about divorce. They seem to give an abbreviated summary of his teaching, of which Matthew records a fuller version in chapter 19. We shall be wise to take the two passages together and to interpret the shorter in the light of the longer.

We know that at the time of Christ a controversy about divorce was being conducted between the rival rabbinic schools of Hillel and Shammai. Rabbi Shammai took a rigorist line and taught from Deuteronomy 24:1 that the sole ground for divorce was some grave matrimonial offense, something evidently "unseemly" or "indecent." Rabbi Hillel, on the other hand, held a very lax view. Hillel, arguing that the ground for divorce was something "unseemly," interpreted this term in the widest possible way to include a wife's most trivial offenses. If she proved to be an incompetent cook, or if he lost interest in her because of her plain looks and because he became enamored of some other more beautiful woman, these things were "unseemly" and justified him divorcing her. The Pharisees seem to have been attracted by Rabbi Hillel's laxity, which will explain the form their question took: "Is it lawful for a man to divorce his wife *for any and every reason?*" (Matthew 19:3, emphasis added). In other words, they wanted to know whose side Jesus was on in the contemporary debate, and whether he belonged to the school of rigorism or of laxity.

Our Lord's reply to their question was in three parts. It is revealing to consider these separately and in the order in which he spoke them. In each he dissented from the Pharisees.

1. *The Pharisees were preoccupied with the grounds for divorce, Jesus with the institution of marriage.* Jesus' reply to the Pharisees was not a reply. He declined to answer their question. Instead, he asked a counterquestion about their reading of Scripture. He referred them back to Genesis, both to the creation of humanity as male and female (Genesis 1) and to the institution of marriage (Genesis 2) by which a man leaves his parents and is united to his wife, and the two become one. This biblical definition implies that marriage is both exclusive and permanent. It is these two aspects of marriage that Jesus selects for emphasis (Matthew 19:6). Thus marriage, according to our Lord's exposition of its origins, is a divine institution by which God makes permanently one two people who decisively and publicly leave their parents in order to form a new unit of society and then "become one flesh" (Genesis 2:24).

2. *The Pharisees called Moses' provision for divorce a command; Jesus called it a concession to the hardness of human hearts.* The Pharisees responded to Jesus' exposition of the institution of marriage by asking, "Why then did Moses command that a man give his wife a certificate of divorce and send her away?" (Matthew 19:7). Jesus' quotation of scribal teaching in the Sermon on the Mount was similar: "It has been said, 'Anyone who divorces his wife must give her a certificate of divorce'" (Matthew 5:31). Both these were garbled versions of the Mosaic provision, typical of the Pharisees' disregard for what Scripture really said and implied. A careful reading of Deuteronomy 24:1-4 reveals something quite different. To begin with, the whole paragraph hinges on a long series of conditional clauses. *If . . . if . . . if . . . then.* The thrust of

the passage is to prohibit remarriage to one's own divorced partner. That prohibition (Deuteronomy 24:4) is the only command in the whole passage. There is certainly no command to a husband to divorce his wife, nor even any encouragement to do so. There is only a reference to certain necessary procedures *if* a divorce takes place; therefore at the very most a reluctant permission is implied and a current practice is tolerated.

How, then, did Jesus respond to the Pharisees' question about the regulation of Moses? He attributed it to the hardness of people's hearts. In so doing he did not deny that the regulation was from God. He implied, however, that it was not a divine instruction but only a divine concession to human weakness. "Moses permitted you. . . . But it was not this way from the beginning" (Matthew 19:8). Thus even the divine concession was in principle inconsistent with the divine intention.

3. The Pharisees regarded divorce lightly; Jesus took it so seriously that, with only one exception, he called all remarriage after divorce adultery. Since God instituted marriage as an exclusive and permanent union, which he makes and humans must not break, Jesus draws the inevitable deduction that to divorce one's partner and marry another, or to marry a divorced person, is to enter a forbidden, adulterous relationship. For the person who may have secured a divorce in the eyes of human law is still in the eyes of God married to his or her first partner. Only one exception is made to this principle: *except for sexual immorality* (Matthew 5:32; 19:9). We must accept this "exceptive clause" not only as a genuine part of Matthew's Gospel (for no manuscripts omit it) but also as an authentic word of Jesus. Under Mosaic law adultery was punishable by death (although the death penalty for this offense seems to have fallen into disuse by the time of Jesus); so nobody would have questioned that marital unfaithfulness was a just ground for divorce.

The next question about the exceptive clause concerns what is meant by *sexual immorality*. The Greek word is *porneia*, derived from *pornē*, a prostitute, without specifying whether she or her client is married or unmarried. Further, it is used in the Septuagint for the unfaithfulness of Israel, Yahweh's bride, as exemplified in Hosea's wife Gomer. It means "unchastity," some act of physical sexual immorality. Jesus was saying that the only situation in which divorce and remarriage are possible without breaking the seventh commandment is when it has already been broken by some serious sexual sin.

Nevertheless the matter cannot be left there. This reluctant permission of Jesus must still be seen for what it is: a continued accommodation to the hardness of human hearts. In addition, it must always be read both in its immediate context (Christ's emphatic endorsement of the permanence of marriage in God's purpose) and also in the wider context of the Sermon on the Mount and of the whole Bible, which proclaim a gospel of reconciliation. So one must never begin a discussion on this subject by inquiring about the legitimacy of divorce. To be preoccupied with the grounds for divorce is to be guilty of the very Pharisaism which Jesus condemned.

If the rabbis tended to be permissive in their attitude to divorce, they were permissive also in their teaching about oaths. We must look first at the Mosaic law, then at the Pharisaic distortion and finally at the true implication of the law on which Jesus insisted. "Again, you have heard that it was said to the people long ago, 'Do not break your oath, but fulfill to the Lord the vows you have made'" (Matthew 5:33). This is not an accurate quotation of any one law of Moses. At the same time, it is a not inaccurate summary of several Old Testament precepts which require people who make vows to keep them. The vows in question are, strictly speaking, oaths in which the speakers call upon God to witness their vows and to punish them if they break them.

The Pharisees shifted people's attention from the vow itself and the need to keep it to the formula used in making it. They developed elaborate rules for the taking of vows. They listed which formulae were permissible, and they added that only those formulae which included the divine name made the vow binding. One need not be so particular, they said, about keeping vows in which the divine name had not been used. Jesus expressed his contempt for this kind of sophistry in one of the "woes" against the Pharisees which Matthew records later (Matthew 23:16-22).

In the Sermon on the Mount, Jesus begins by arguing that the question of the formula used in making vows is a total irrelevance, and in particular that the Pharisees' distinction between formulae which mention God and those which do not is entirely artificial. However hard you try, Jesus said, you cannot avoid some reference to God, for the whole world is God's world and you cannot eliminate him from any of it. Since anybody who makes a vow must keep it, strictly speaking all formulae are superfluous. A vow is binding irrespective of its accompanying formula. The real implication of the law is that we must keep our promises and be people of our word. Then vows become unnecessary.

If divorce is due to human hard-heartedness, swearing is due to human untruthfulness. Both were permitted by the law; neither was commanded; neither should be necessary.

What's the main idea in this section?

What is one thing you can act on based on this reading?

PART 4. DISCUSS
Putting It All Together

OPEN
Your group has been asked to write a chapter for a book on marriage. The title you've been given for your chapter is "The Top Ten Reasons Why Marriages Fail." What reasons will you give for the breakup of marriages?

READ MATTHEW 5:31-37; 19:3-9.
There is almost no unhappiness so painful as that of an unhappy marriage. And there is almost no tragedy as great as when a relationship God meant for love and fulfillment degenerates into a nonrelationship of bitterness, discord and despair.

1. As a group, discuss your answers to question one of part one: How do Jesus' statements contrast with the questions about divorce that he was asked by the Pharisees?

2. This Scripture passage covers the subjects of faithfulness in marriage and in speech. What is the connection between marriage and keeping promises?

3. What was the real purpose of Moses' instructions about the certificate of divorce?

4. What do you derive from Genesis 2:18-25 about God's purposes in marriage?

5. What are some contemporary pressures on Christian marriages?

6. Why do you think divorce (not necessarily among Christians) has become more common?

7. Jesus' teaching in Matthew 5:31-32 makes it clear that he stands against divorce. Why do you think he allows the exception for sexual immorality (Matthew 5:32)?

8. How does honesty in our dealings with each other glorify God?

9. What did people hope to accomplish when they swore by the name of the Lord or by such things as heaven, the earth or Jerusalem?

10. Think of a time when you made a promise and did not keep it. Do you now wish you had not promised anything at all, or do you still think the promise was a good idea? Explain your answer.

11. Why should taking an oath be unnecessary for Christians?

12. Do you think you are becoming more or less honest in your speech, and why?

Pray for faithfulness in marriage or singleness and for faithfulness to your word.

SESSION SIX

How to Really Love Your Enemies

Matthew 5:38-48

WHERE WE'RE GOING

This passage brings us to the highest point of the Sermon on the Mount, for which it is both most admired and most resented. Christ calls us to show our attitude of total love to an "evil person" (v. 39) and our "enemies" (v. 44). Nowhere is the challenge of the Sermon greater. Nowhere is the distinctness of the Christian counterculture more obvious. Nowhere is our need of the power of the Holy Spirit (whose first fruit is love) more compelling.

> Part 1. Investigate: Matthew 5:38-48 (On Your Own)
>
> Part 2. Connect: Scripture to Scripture (On Your Own)
>
> Part 3. Reflect: A Christian's Righteousness: *Non-Retaliation and Active Love* (On Your Own)
>
> Part 4. Discuss: Putting It All Together (With a Group)

A PRAYER TO PRAY

Here's a prayer you can use to set you on your way:

Merciful God, you are the source of all love and kindness. We believe the Scripture which says "God is love." On the other hand, in our natural selves, we are selfish and spiteful and we want our own way. Change our hearts so that we love those who seem unlovable and so that we do good to our enemies, not outwardly for show, but inwardly from our renewed hearts. We boldly ask this in the name of the one who kept praying "Father, forgive them." Amen.

PART 1. INVESTIGATE
Matthew 5:38-48

Read Matthew 5:38-48.

1. What do you find most difficult about Jesus' instructions in these verses?

2. Jesus' quotation of "Eye for eye, and tooth for tooth" comes from Exodus 21:24. How would this instruction to Israel's judges clarify the meaning of justice?

How would it also limit the extent of revenge?

3. The Pharisees evidently extended this principle from the law courts (where it belonged) to the realm of personal relationships (where it did not belong). What consequences might have resulted?

4. Looking at verses 39-42, how would you contrast our natural responses in such situations with the responses Jesus expects of us?

5:38. *"Eye for an eye" and "tooth for a tooth" are part of the widespread ancient Near Eastern law of retaliation. In Israel and other cultures, this principle was enforced by a court and refers to legalized vengeance; personal vengeance was never accepted in the law of Moses, except as a concession for a relative's murder (Num 35:18-21). The Old Testament did not permit personal vengeance; David, a great warrior, recognized this principle (1 Sam 25:33; 26:10-11).*

5:39. *The blow on the right cheek was the most grievous insult possible in the ancient world (apart from inflicting serious physical harm), and in many cultures was listed alongside the "eye for an eye" laws; both Jewish and Roman law permitted prosecution for this offense. A prophet might endure such ill treatment (1 Kings 22:24; Is 50:6).*

5:40. *The poorest people of the Empire (e.g., most peasants in Egypt) had only an inner and outer garment, and the theft of a cloak would lead to legal recourse. Jesus gives this advice in* *spite of the fact that, under Jewish law, a legal case to regain one's cloak would have been foolproof: a creditor could not take a poor person's outer cloak, which might serve as one's only blanket at night as well as a coat (Ex 22:26-27).*

5. What is accomplished by turning the other cheek or going a second mile?

6. In what situations might Christ's commands apply today?

5:41. *Roman soldiers had the legal right to impress the labor, work animal or substance of local residents (cf. Mk 15:21).*

The Jewish hierarchy favored the status quo with Rome; some revolutionaries wanted to revolt. Most Palestinian Jews in this period wanted freedom but were not revolutionaries. But by A.D. 66 Jewish Palestine was caught up in a war, and by 70 the wisdom of Jesus' course was evident: Rome won the war, and the Jewish people, led to defeat by the revolutionaries, were crushed.

7. According to Jesus, how are we to treat our enemies and why (vv. 44-45)?

8. In what ways is Jesus' command extraordinary (vv. 46-48)?

5:42. *Beggars were widespread. The Bible stressed giving to those in need (Deut 15:11; Ps 112:5, 9; Prov 21:13). God would take care of the needs of those who helped the poor (Deut 15:10; Prov 19:17; 22:9; 28:8). Biblical laws against usury and especially about lending to the poor before the year of release (Deut 15:9; every seventh year debts were to be forgiven; cf. Lev 25)*

9. Does all this mean that Christians are to be doormats for the world to walk on? Explain.

10. How was Jesus himself an example of the principles "Do not resist an evil person" and "Love your enemies"?

support Jesus' principle here, but Jesus goes even farther in emphasizing unselfish giving (especially Lk 6:35).

11. How might you reflect your Father's character when you are mistreated?

Pray for God's blessing on people who have mistreated you or been your enemy.

5:43-44. *The Old Testament did not explicitly teach hatred for one's enemies (Ex 23:4-5; Prov 25:21-22), although hating God's enemies was a pious way to feel (Ps 139:19-22); some Jewish groups, like the Essenes, emphasized hatred toward those outside the covenant. Greek ethics sometimes stressed learning from one's enemies' criticism but also could stress making sure to hurt one's enemies more than one was hurt by them (so Isocrates, a fourth-century B.C. Athenian orator and rhetorician).*

5:48. *Matthew 5:48 summarizes 5:21-47. The Aramaic word for "perfect" can mean "complete" or "whole," including the nuance of "merciful" (Lk 6:36); in this context, it means fulfilling the requirements of Matthew 5:21-47. The Bible already commanded being holy as God is holy (Lev 11:44-45; 19:2; 20:26), and Judaism (as well as some Greek philosophers) sometimes argued ethics on the basis of imitating God's character.*

PART 2. CONNECT
Scripture to Scripture

AN EYE FOR AN EYE

"An eye for an eye and a tooth for a tooth" is a cliché for revenge. A common retort is that if we practice such retribution, the whole world will be blind and toothless.

Many people do not realize that the phrase comes from the Bible. Those of us who do know where it comes from often wish that it weren't there. How do we explain such apparently vicious instructions from God in a book which is supposed to be filled with love? Or is this an example of the wrath of the "God of the Old Testament," in contrast to the love of Jesus in the New Testament?

When you hear the phrase "an eye for an eye and a tooth for a tooth," how do you react? Check all that apply:

___ a. It's a cruel form of punishment.

___ b. It's outmoded and doesn't apply today.

___ c. It means the punishment should fit the crime.

___ d. It's a form of revenge.

___ e. It limits punishment to what's fair.

___ f. It might start a cycle that never ends.

When we read the law of retribution in Scripture, it may be hard for us to see it as anything but permission for vengeance. But God laid out different, specific instructions regarding vengeance so that the Israelites wouldn't confuse the two.

Read Leviticus 19:18 and fill in the blanks in the following statement:

God said that _____ should not take vengeance, but that only

_____ has the right of vengeance.

What, then, do we make of the Old Testament law of retribution mentioned in Matthew 5? The rabbis whom Jesus quoted in Matthew 5:38 had the quotation right. Read Exodus 21:22-25, which is the first occurrence of the biblical law of exact retribution. What are the particular circumstances under which this law was to be applied?

_____

_____

_____

_____

How does Leviticus 24:17-22 broaden the application of the law of exact retribution?

_____

_____

_____

_____

Read Deuteronomy 19:15-21. What are the circumstances in this case under which "life for life, eye for eye, tooth for tooth, hand for hand, foot for foot" are to be exacted?

_____

_____

_____

_____

How does Deuteronomy 19:17-19 limit the people who can exact such penalties?

_____

_____

_____

_____

The law of exact retribution was designed to limit punishment to what was appropriate for the wrong. If someone knocked out your tooth or made you lose an eye or a foot, you did not have the right to kill the person. In fact, you did not have the right to take retribution at all; that was left to the judges appointed by the Lord. As scholar Walter Kaiser explains, "While some have thought that this text condoned excessive retribution, it actually curbed all retribution and any personal retaliation among Israel's citizens."[1]

In addition, though the law of exact retribution may sound harsh to us, it was actually a radical digression from the customs and laws of the people groups surrounding Israel. Craig Blomberg, similar to Kaiser, notes that "the original purpose of this Hebrew legislation probably was to limit the amount of revenge that could be exacted for an offense and to limit the location of that exaction to a court of law. . . . Many other ancient Near Eastern cultures," he goes on to point out, "were often not even this humane."[2]

Other Old Testament laws go further still, calling for even more mercy in a kind of inexact retribution. For example, immediately after the law about injury to a pregnant woman, there is a law about injury to a slave—one of the lowest members of Israelite society. Read Exodus 21:26-27. Respond to the following questions as true or false:

_____ If an owner hits a slave and the slave loses an eye or a tooth as a result, the owner must lose an eye or a tooth.

_____ A slave owner who causes a slave to lose an eye or a tooth has to free that slave.

_____ If a slave owner causes injury to a slave, the slave is allowed to take vengeance.

_____ A monetary value is placed on a slave's eye or tooth but not on the owner's eye or tooth.

_____ A slave who attacked his or her owner had to suffer retribution.

In his gracious laws restraining personal vengeance, God challenged the Israelites to be slow to anger and to develop a more merciful and humane character. In this way their society would be radically different from the nations around them. Israel's national life was to reflect the merciful character of their God.

HOW TO TREAT AN ENEMY

None of us wants enemies. And yet, in the Sermon on the Mount, Jesus seemed to assume that his hearers would have enemies, like it or not. The Old Testament is hard to read in this regard; when Israel entered Canaan, for example, God instructed them to wipe out their enemies. But there was a reason for the command.

The Canaanites are known from modern Near Eastern studies to have been utterly corrupt in religion and culture. So nauseating were their abominable practices that God said, "Even the land was defiled; so I punished it for its sin, and the land vomited out its inhabitants" (Leviticus 18:25). Indeed, if Israel were to follow their customs, she would share their fate: "And if you defile the land, it will vomit you out as it vomited out the nations that were before you" (Leviticus 18:28).

When it came to personal enemies, the Old Testament had equally strong words, but this time they were words about showing mercy. Read Exodus 23:4-5 and Deuteronomy 22:1-4.

Who is the beneficiary in Exodus 23:4-5?

_____

_____

_____

_____

Who is the beneficiary in Deuteronomy 22:1-4?

_____

_____

_____

_____

What do you learn from the fact that the people to be helped are very different, but the help to be given is the same?

_____

_____

_____

_____

Read Proverbs 25:21-22. Fill in the missing parts of the passage:

"If _____ is hungry, give _____;

    if _____, give him _____.

In doing this, you will heap burning coals on his head,

    and the LORD will _____."

There have been various interpretations of the "burning coals," none of which are conclusive, but the first part of the passage is clear. None of us wants enemies, but if we do find ourselves with an enemy, we are to minister to the needs of that person. What would be a practical example of carrying out verse 21?

THE MESSIAH DOES NOT RETALIATE

For many centuries the Jews expected their Messiah to come. Most of them anticipated a military ruler who would crush their enemies. Those who studied the Scriptures with an open mind, however, should have seen that this great figure would actually be a suffering Messiah. He would be abused by his enemies and would refrain from retaliation or revenge. He would willingly give up his own life and allow others to nail him to a cross because it was God's will for the Messiah's life to be the perfect sacrifice for sin.

Read Isaiah 52:13–53:12. This picture of the Lord's servant is accepted by Christians as a prophecy of the coming Messiah. Match up the qualities of the Messiah with the corresponding Isaiah passage.

Isaiah 52:14	despised, rejected, held in low esteem
Isaiah 53:2	led like lamb to slaughter, was silent
Isaiah 53:3	no beauty or majesty, not desirable
Isaiah 53:4-6	disfigured appearance
Isaiah 53:7	poured out his life for sin
Isaiah 53:12	bore our suffering, transgressions, iniquities

How would the Messiah be the perfect embodiment of the mercy that had been expressed in God's laws?

_____

_____

_____

_____

---

[1]Walter Kaiser Jr., Peter H. Davids, F. F. Bruce and Manfred Brauch, *Hard Sayings of the Bible* (Downers Grove, IL: InterVarsity Press, 1996), p. 151.

[2]Craig L. Blomberg, "Matthew," in *Commentary on the New Testament Use of the Old Testament,* ed. G. K. Beale and D. A. Carson (Grand Rapids: Baker Academic, 2007), pp. 26-27.

A Christian's Righteousness

NON-RETALIATION AND ACTIVE LOVE

The excerpt from the oral teaching of the rabbis which Jesus quoted comes straight out of the Mosaic law (Exodus 21:24). As we consider it, we need to remember that the law of Moses was a civil as well as a moral code. The context makes it clear beyond question that this was an instruction to the judges of Israel. It expressed the *lex talionis*, the principle of an exact retribution, the purpose of which was both to lay the foundation of justice, specifying the punishment which a wrongdoer deserved, and to limit the compensation of the victim to an exact equivalent and no more. It thus had the double effect of defining justice and restraining revenge.

It is almost certain that by the time of Jesus, literal retaliation for damage had been replaced in Jewish legal practice by money penalties or "damages." But the scribes and Pharisees evidently extended this principle of just retribution from the law courts (where it belongs) to the realm of personal relationships (where it does not belong). They used it to justify personal revenge, although the law explicitly forbade this: "Do not seek revenge or bear a grudge against anyone among your people" (Leviticus 19:18).

In his reply Jesus did not contradict the principle of retribution, for it is a true and just principle. What Jesus affirmed in the antithesis was rather that this principle, though it pertains to the law courts and to the judgment of God, is not applicable to our personal relationships. These are to be based on love, not justice. Our duty to individuals who wrong us is not retaliation, but the acceptance of injustice without revenge of redress: "Do not resist an evil person" (Matthew 5:39).

But what exactly is the meaning of this call to non-resistance? The Greek verb *anthistēmi* is plain: it is to resist, withstand or set oneself against someone or something. The first clue to a correct understanding of Jesus' teaching is to recognize that the words *tō ponērō* ("the evil") are masculine not neuter. What we are forbidden to resist is not evil as such, evil in the abstract, nor "the evil one" meaning the devil, but an evil person, *one who is evil*.

The four mini-illustrations which follow all apply the principle of Christian non-retaliation and indicate the lengths to which it must go. Each introduces a person who is in some sense "evil" who seeks to do us an injury. In each of the four situations, Jesus said, our Christian duty is so completely to forbear revenge that we even allow the "evil" person to double the injury.

Jesus' illustrations and personal example do not depict a weakling who offers no resistance. Rather, they depict a strong person whose self-control and love for others are so powerful that the person rejects absolutely every conceivable form of retaliation.

However conscientious we may be in our determination not to sidestep the implications of Jesus' teaching, we cannot take the four little cameos with wooden, unimaginative literalism. This is partly because they are given not as detailed regulations but as illustrations of a principle, and partly because they must be seen to uphold the principle they are intended to illustrate. That principle is love, the selfless love of a person who refuses to take revenge but instead studies the highest welfare of the other person and of society, and reacts accordingly.

Thus the only limit to the Christian's generosity will be a limit which love itself may impose. For example, the apostle Paul once "resisted" (same Greek word) the apostle Peter to his face (Galatians 2:11-14). Peter's behavior had been wrong, evil. He had withdrawn from fellowship with Gentile brothers and so contradicted the gospel. Paul opposed him, publicly rebuking him and denouncing his action. And I think we must defend Paul's conduct as a true expression of love. For on the one hand Paul had no personal animosity toward Peter, while on the other there was a strong love for the Gentile Christians Peter had affronted and for the gospel he had denied.

Similarly, Christ's illustrations are not to be taken as the charter for any unscrupulous tyrant, ruffian, beggar or thug. His purpose was to forbid revenge, not to encourage injustice, dishonesty or vice. Christ teaches not the irresponsibility which encourages evil but the forbearance which renounces revenge. Authentic Christian nonresistance is nonretaliation.

We cannot take Jesus' command "Do not resist an evil person" as an absolute prohibition of the use of all force (including the police) unless we are prepared to say that the Bible contradicts itself and that the apostles misunderstood Jesus. For the New Testament teaches that the state is a divine institution, commissioned both to punish the wrongdoer and to reward those who do good (Romans 13:1-7). Rather, Scripture's prohibition of vengeance is not because retribution is in itself wrong, but because it is the prerogative of God, not human beings; Jesus was not prohibiting the administration of justice, but rather forbidding us to take the law into our own hands. "An eye for an eye" is a principle of justice belonging to courts of law. In personal life we must be rid not only of all retaliation in word and deed, but of all animosity of spirit.

In Matthew 5:43-48, Jesus puts out another antithesis. We have already seen how blatant a perversion of the law is the instruction "Love your neighbor and hate your enemy" (Matthew 5:43) because of what it omits from the

commandment and adds to it. It deliberately narrows both the standard of love, leaving out the crucial words "as yourself" (Leviticus 19:18), and love's objects, qualifying the category of "neighbor" by specifically excluding enemies and adding the command to hate them instead.

"My neighbor," the rabbis argued, "is one of my own people, a fellow Jew, who belongs to my race and my religion. The law says nothing about strangers or enemies. So, since the command is to love only my neighbor, it must be taken as a permission, even an injunction, to hate my enemy. For my enemy is not my neighbor whom I am to love." The reasoning is rational enough to convince those who wanted to be convinced and to confirm them in their own racial prejudice. But they evidently ignored the instruction earlier in the same chapter to leave the gleanings of field and vineyard "for the poor and the foreigner" (Leviticus 19:10) and the unequivocal statement against racial discrimination at the end of the chapter: "The foreigner residing among you must be treated as your native-born. Love them as yourself, for you were foreigners in Egypt. I am the LORD your God" (Leviticus 19:34). Similarly, "The same law applies both to the native-born and to the foreigner residing among you" (Exodus 12:49).

The rabbis' words "and hate your enemy" had no business being added to God's law. God did not teach his people a double standard of morality, one for a neighbor and another for an enemy.

So Jesus contradicted their addition as a gross distortion of the law: "But I tell you, love your enemies" (Matthew 5:44). For our neighbor, as he later illustrated in the parable of the good Samaritan, is not necessarily a member of our own race, rank or religion. Our "neighbor" in the vocabulary of God includes our enemy. What makes the person our neighbor is simply that the person is a fellow human being in need, whose need we know and are in a position in some measure to relieve.

True love is not sentiment so much as service—practical, humble, sacrificial service. Our enemy is seeking our harm; we must seek our enemy's good. For this is how God has treated us. It was "while we were God's enemies" that Christ died for us to reconcile us to God (Romans 5:10). If he gave himself for his enemies, we must give ourselves for ours.

Part of loving our enemies is to "pray for those who persecute you" (Matthew 5:44). If intercessory prayer is an expression of what love we have, it is a means to increase our love as well. It is impossible to pray for someone without loving the person, and impossible to go on praying without discovering that our love for the person grows and matures.

Jesus seems to have prayed for his executioners even as the iron spikes were being driven through his hands and feet; indeed the imperfect tense suggests that he kept praying, kept repeating his entreaty "Father, forgive them, for they do not know what they are doing" (Luke 23:34). If the cruel torture of crucifixion could not silence our Lord's prayer for his enemies, what pain, pride, prejudice or sloth could justify the silencing of ours?

Having indicated that our love for our enemies will express itself in deeds, words and prayers, Jesus goes on to declare that only then shall we prove conclusively whose children we are, for only then shall we be exhibiting a love like the love of our heavenly father (Matthew 5:45). Divine love is indiscriminate love, shown equally to good people and bad.

Fallen human beings are not incapable of loving. The doctrine of total depravity does not mean that original sin has rendered people incapable of doing anything good at all, but rather that every good they do is tainted to some degree by evil. We Christians are specifically called to love our enemies (in which love there is no self-interest), and this is impossible without the supernatural grace of God.

If we love only those who love us, if we greet only our fellow Christians, Jesus asks, "What are you doing more than others?" (Matthew 5:47). It is not enough for Christians to *resemble* non-Christians; our calling is to outstrip them in virtue. Our righteousness is to *surpass* that of the Pharisees and teachers of the law (Matthew 5:20) and our love is to be *more than* (Matthew 5:47) that of the pagans.

This "super-love" is not the love of human beings, but the love of God, who in common grace gives sun and rain to the wicked. The model Jesus sets before us as an alternative to the world around us is our Father above us. "Be perfect, therefore, as your heavenly Father is perfect" (Matthew 5:48). The concept that God's people must imitate God rather than other people is not new. The book of Leviticus repeats some five times as a refrain the command "I am the LORD your God; . . . therefore be holy, because I am holy" (Leviticus 11:44-45). Yet here Christ's call to us is not to be *holy* but to be *perfect*.

The words of Jesus cannot be pressed into meaning that we can reach a state of sinless perfection in this life. Jesus has already indicated in the Beatitudes that a hunger and thirst after righteousness is a perpetual characteristic of his disciples (Matthew 5:6), and in the next chapter he will teach us to pray constantly for forgiveness (Matthew 6:12). Clearly Jesus did not expect his followers to become morally perfect in this life. The context shows that the "perfection" he means relates to love, the perfect love of God which is shown even to those who do not return it.

Christ's call to us is new, not only because it is a command to be "perfect" rather than "holy," but also because of his description of the God we are to imitate. In the Old Testament it was always "I am the LORD, who brought you up out of Egypt to be your God; therefore be holy, because I am holy" (Leviticus 11:45). But now in New Testament days it is not the unique Redeemer of Israel whom we are to follow and obey; it is our "Father in heaven," our "heavenly Father" (Matthew 5:45, 48). Our obedience will come from our hearts as the manifestation of our new nature.

Looking back over all six antitheses in Matthew 5:21-48, it has become clear what the greater righteousness is to which Christians are summoned. It is a deep inward righteousness of the heart where the Holy Spirit has written God's law. This righteousness, whether expressed in purity, honesty or charity, will show to whom we belong. Our Christian calling is to imitate not the world but the Father. And it is by this imitation of him that the Christian counterculture becomes visible.

What's the main idea in this section?

What is one thing you can act on based on this reading?

PART 4. DISCUSS
Putting It All Together

OPEN

When have you found it difficult to forgive another person?

READ MATTHEW 5:38-48.

The real test of love does not come in how we relate to the kind and lovable but in how we relate to the cruel and despicable.

1. What was the purpose of the "eye for eye, tooth for tooth" law of exact retribution?

2. As a group, discuss your answers to question ten from part one: How was Jesus himself an example of the principles "Do not resist an evil person" and "Love your enemies"?

3. From the reading in the "Reflect" section, how do you explain the fact that unbelievers can do good things and can be loving?

4. How does loving and praying for our enemies display our relationship as children of God?

5. What did you glean from the reading about what Jesus meant by "perfect" (v. 48)?

6. What do you find most difficult about Jesus' instructions in these verses?

7. When has someone turned the other cheek, handed over the coat or gone the second mile for you, and with what results?

   How do you sense the Holy Spirit urging you to do the same now for someone else?

8. Think of people (both individuals and groups) you find easy to love and welcome; think also of those you find difficult to love and welcome. Why do you think you respond to each person/group as you do?

9. How can Christians do "more than others" in the sense of verses 46-47?

10. What is one idea from question nine that you and your group can put into practice this week?

Pray that your lives will increasingly reflect your relationship with your Father in heaven.

SESSION SEVEN

How Not to Be Religious

Matthew 6:1-6, 16-18

WHERE WE'RE GOING

In Matthew 5 Jesus taught us that our righteousness must be greater than that of the Pharisees (because they obeyed the letter of the law, while our obedience must include our heart) and greater also than that of the pagans (because they love each other, while our love must include our enemies as well). Now in Matthew 6 Jesus draws the same two contrasts regarding our religion. He says that we should not be hypocritical like the Pharisees and not mechanical like the pagans.

Part 1. Investigate: Matthew 6:1-6, 16-18 (On Your Own)

Part 2. Connect: Scripture to Scripture (On Your Own)

Part 3. Reflect: A Christian's Religion: *Not Hypocritical but Real* (On Your Own)

Part 4. Discuss: Putting It All Together (With a Group)

A PRAYER TO PRAY

Here's a prayer you can use as you begin your study:

God of truth and love, you are always honest with us. You often tell us what we do not want to hear. By your grace we want to be honest with you and with each other. Although it is frightening to pray this, show us our hypocrisy. Forgive us for our selfish craving for the praise of other people. Help us to want only your praise in these sensitive areas of giving, praying and fasting. Help us also to see practical ways to carry out these responsibilities in the sincere motive of love for you and others. Amen.

PART 1. INVESTIGATE
Matthew 6:1-6, 16-18

Read Matthew 6:1-6 and 16-18.

6:1. *This verse is the thesis statement that introduces the three examples of private piety in 6:2-16. Judaism stressed that one should not perform deeds for the sake of reward but nonetheless promised reward, as Jesus does here; this reward is rendered at the day of judgment, as in Judaism. Prayer, fasting and gifts to the poor were basic components of Jewish piety (Tobit 12:8), and many rabbis listed qualities (e.g., virtues on which the world was founded) in sets of three.*

1. Jesus illustrates the principle of verse 1 by focusing on three religious practices: giving, praying and fasting. What images come to mind when you read about the hypocrites in verse 2?

2. In verse 1 Jesus commands us "not to practice your righteousness in front of others to be seen by them." Yet in 5:16 he said, "Let your light shine before others, that they may see your good deeds." Is there a contradiction here? Explain.

3. What does Jesus mean when he says, "When you give to the needy, do not let your left hand know what your right hand is doing" (v. 3)?

6:2-4. *Greeks and Romans did not support personal charity; wealthy contributions to public projects or to poorer clients were meant to secure the giver's popularity. In contrast, charity was central to Jewish piety; some writers even said that it saved a person, although later Jewish laws technically did not permit one to give over 20 percent above his tithes.*

Why is this important (vv. 2, 4)?

Some commentators have taken the trumpet sounding literally, but it is hyperbolic (people did not blow trumpets when giving alms) and may reflect a play on words (charity boxes were often shaped like trumpets). Not letting one's left hand know about the right hand's

4. In what ways are we tempted to be hypocritical in our giving?

5. What was wrong with the way hypocrites prayed in Jesus' day (v. 5)?

6. In what ways do hypocrites pray today?

7. Why and how is our praying to be different (v. 6)?

8. How do you think the reward the Father will give us (v. 6) differs from the reward we receive from others (v. 5)?

9. In verse 16 Jesus assumes Christians will fast (although few of us do). Why and how should we fast (vv. 16-18)?

10. Fasting was a way that people were trying to seek the approval of others. In what other areas are we tempted to seek the approval of people rather than of God?

11. How can this passage help to purify our motives?

Ask God to help you focus on him (rather than yourself) as you worship.

---

gift is clearly hyperbole. The language of "having" a reward "in full" is the language of repayment in ancient business receipts.

6:5-6. *The problem is not public prayer but motives directed toward other people rather than toward God. It was probably common for pious people to recite their prayers individually in the synagogue; it is not clear that everyone prayed simultaneously in all synagogues as early as Jesus' time. The "room" could have been a storeroom; most people did not have private rooms in their houses, and only that room would have a door on it. Standing was a common posture for prayer.*

6:16-18. *During at least the dry seasons, many of the most pious people fasted (without water, though this was unhealthy) two particular days a week. This fasting was considered meritorious, although ascetic fasting (e.g., fasting only to "beat down the flesh") was forbidden. Jewish fasting required abstinence not only from food but also from other pleasures, which would include the usual practice of anointing one's head with oil to prevent dry skin; avoiding all these practices made fasting obvious.*

PART 2. CONNECT
Scripture to Scripture

In this section of the Sermon on the Mount, Jesus focused on the motivations for three practices: giving to the needy, praying and fasting.

GIVING TO THE NEEDY

The Old Testament is full of encouragements to be generous to people in need. The responsibility is firmly linked to the Lord's own concern for the poor and the fact that he approves of such generosity.

The Torah includes laws specifically aimed at helping poor people in the agricultural economy of Israel. Read the following Scriptures and match up each reference with the instructions it contains about how the needy people in the land were to be provided for.

special tithe every three years	Exodus 22:25-27
leave some of the harvest for gleaners	Deuteronomy 14:28-29 and 26:12
pay a poor person's wages by day's end	Deuteronomy 15:7-11
no interest or security for a loan to a poor person	Deuteronomy 24:14-15
lend freely even though the sabbath year for canceling debts is near	Deuteronomy 24:19-22

What do these laws have in common with regard to the dignity of the poor?

_____

_____

_____

_____

As compassionate as these laws sound, even perfect obedience to them would not necessarily reflect true concern for the poor. A person could outwardly practice everything these laws demanded but still inwardly feel scorn for less fortunate people. The Old Testament, however, like Jesus in Matthew 6, points God's people toward genuine giving and promises a reward from our Father for giving that comes from the heart.

Read the following proverbs. What is said in each one about the person who is genuinely kind and generous to the poor?

Proverbs 14:21: _____

Proverbs 14:31: _____

Proverbs 19:17: _____

Proverbs 22:9: _____

Proverbs 28:8: _____

Proverbs 28:27: _____

If our giving should be unselfish and openhanded, why do you think these Scriptures promise such great blessings for the giver?

_____

_____

_____

_____

PRAYING

The Old Testament is full of prayers. The first recorded prayer in Scripture—that is, the first time we overhear a person talking to God—is Adam's frightened response to God's question "Where are you?" Adam replies "I heard you in the garden, and I was afraid because I was naked; so I hid" (Genesis 3:9-10).

It is remarkable that although sin had just thrown a terrible wall between God and humanity, prayer was still possible. Human beings could still talk to God, and God would answer.

The Old Testament records several dramatic and eloquent public prayers, notably Solomon's prayer at the dedication of the temple in Jerusalem (1 Kings 8:22-60) and the Levites' prayer at the reading of the law in the rebuilt city of Jerusalem (Nehemiah 9:1-38). Other Old Testament prayers are one-on-one conversations between an individual and the Lord, often in urgent circumstances.

For example, Genesis contains a particularly urgent prayer of Jacob, spoken in a time of personal crisis. After he cheated his twin brother, Esau, out of his birthright and his blessing, their mother, Rebekah, warned him that Esau was plotting to kill him. She advised him to flee to the home of her brother Laban in Paddan Aram. Jacob did so and stayed for twenty years, accumulating a large family and considerable wealth. After twenty years he and his family left to return to Canaan. As they approached Edom, where Jacob's brother Esau had settled, Jacob sent messengers ahead with conciliatory gifts for his brother. The messengers returned with word that Esau was coming to meet Jacob.

Jacob divided up the people and the flocks and herds he had with him, thinking that if Esau attacked one group, the rest would escape. Then Jacob prayed. Read Genesis 32:9-12.

Sketch a heart (or any other shape) to represent the heart of Jacob as he prayed this prayer. Inside your sketch, write words and phrases to show what Jacob's prayer reveals about what was in his heart.

What does Jacob's prayer reveal about his relationship with God?

_____

_____

_____

_____

In verse 10 Jacob acknowledges God's goodness to him. How might this acknowledgment have strengthened Jacob's faith even as he prayed?

_____

_____

_____

_____

_____

What would be the value of "reminding" God of his own promises (vv. 9, 13)?

_____

_____

_____

_____

_____

Another example of deeply felt prayer comes in the book of 2 Kings. After the division of the one kingdom of Israel into two, Israel and Judah, the Assyrians invaded and conquered the northern kingdom of Israel. Later another king of Assyria invaded Judah to attempt the same kind of conquest. At that time Hezekiah was king of Judah. The Assyrian commander taunted the people of Jerusalem with the hopelessness of their situation. Hezekiah was in despair, but the prophet Isaiah heartened him. Then the king of Assyria sent Hezekiah a letter ridiculing the God of the Jews. Read how Hezekiah responded in 2 Kings 19:14-19.

If God is everywhere, what would be the significance of Hezekiah taking the letter into the Lord's temple to pray over it?

_____

_____

_____

_____

What does Hezekiah's prayer reveal about his faith in the Lord?

_____

_____

_____

_____

_____

Even as he expressed faith, how was Hezekiah honest about Jerusalem's peril?

_____

_____

_____

_____

_____

How did Hezekiah contrast the gods of the other nations with the Lord, the God of Israel?

Gods of Other Nations   **The Lord, the God of Israel**

What is Hezekiah's aim in praying for deliverance?

_____

_____

_____

_____

_____

The prayers of Jacob and Hezekiah, separated by centuries, are united in their personal intensity. Each prayer shows us one person doing as Jesus instructed in the Sermon on the Mount: secluding himself from distractions and opening his heart before God, in the expectation that God would hear and answer.

FASTING

In the Old Testament, God's people—and occasionally the pagans—fasted for several reasons. Read the following Scriptures and identify the motive for fasting.

2 Chronicles 20:1-4: _____

Ezra 8:15-23: _____

Nehemiah 9:1-3: _____

Jonah 3:1-10: _____

Daniel 9:1-3: _____

At times, people's fasting was apparently in vain; they questioned why God was not paying attention to their outward self-denial. The classic biblical example is in Isaiah 58. Read the chapter and, using the following phrases as prompts, paraphrase what was going on.

The people seemed to be _____.

They asked God why _____.

Through Isaiah, God replied that when they fasted, they _____.

Even while fasting, their behavior toward each other showed that their hearts were _____

_____.

God said that the "fast" he approved of was _____.

A "fast" of the type God described would show that the people _____.

The result of godly fasting would be _____.

As with prayer in the preceding section, genuine fasting is not an external issue. It requires right intentions, which only God can discern. Jesus' words about prayer and fasting in the Sermon on the Mount confirm that "The LORD does not look at the things people look at. People look at the outward appearance, but the LORD looks at the heart" (1 Samuel 16:7).

PART 3. REFLECT
A Christian's Religion
NOT HYPOCRITICAL BUT REAL

Jesus began his instruction on the hill by portraying in the Beatitudes the essential elements of Christian *character* and went on to indicate the *influence* for good which Christians will exert in the community if they exhibit this character. He then described Christian *righteousness* which must exceed the righteousness of the scribes and Pharisees by accepting the full implications of God's law without dodging anything or setting artificial limits.

Jesus now continues his teaching on righteousness, but the emphasis has shifted. Previously "righteousness" related to kindness, purity, honesty and love; now it concerns such practices as almsgiving, praying and fasting. Thus Jesus moves from a Christian's moral righteousness to a Christian's religious righteousness.

It is important to acknowledge that according to Jesus, Christian righteousness has these two dimensions, moral and religious. Some speak and behave as if their major duty as Christians lies in the sphere of religious activity, whether public (churchgoing) or private (devotional exercises). Others react so sharply against such an overemphasis on piety that they talk of a "religionless" Christianity. But there is no need to choose between piety and morality, since Jesus taught that authentic Christian righteousness includes both. In both spheres of righteousness Jesus issues his insistent call to his followers to be different.

At first sight Jesus' words "Be careful not to practice your righteousness in front of others to be seen by them" (Matthew 6:1) appear to contradict his earlier command to "let your light shine before others, that they may see your good deeds" (Matthew 5:16). The explanation lies in the fact that Jesus is speaking against different sins. It is our human coward-ice which made him say "Let your light shine," and it is our human vanity which made him tell us to beware of practicing our piety before others. Our good works must be public so that our light shines; our religious devotions must be secret lest we boast about them. Besides, the end of both instructions of Jesus is the same, namely the glory of God. Why are we to keep our piety secret? It is in order that glory may be given to God, rather than people. Why are we to let our light shine and do good works in the open? It is that people may glorify our heavenly Father.

The three examples of religious righteousness which Jesus gives—almsgiving, praying and fasting—occur in some form in every religion. They are prominent, for example, in the Qur'an. Certainly all Jews were expected to give to the poor, to pray and to fast, and all devout Jews did so. Evidently Jesus expected his disciples to do the same. For he did not begin each paragraph "*If* you give, pray, fast" but "*When* you do so" (see Matthew 6:2, 5, 16).

The three paragraphs follow an identical pattern. In vivid and deliberately humorous imagery Jesus paints a picture of the hypocrite's way of being religious. It is the way of ostentation. Such receive the reward they want, the applause of people. With this he contrasts the Christian way, which is secret, and the only reward which Christians want, the blessing of God who is their heavenly Father and who sees in secret.

1. Christian giving. The Greek word for *almsgiving* in verse 2 means "a deed of mercy or pity." Since our God is a merciful God, as Jesus has just emphasized (Matthew 5:45), his people must be kind and merciful too. Jesus obviously expected his disciples to be generous givers.

Generosity is not enough, however. Our Lord is concerned throughout this sermon with motivation, with the hidden thoughts of the heart. There are three possible motives for our giving. Either we are seeking the praise of people, or we preserve our anonymity but are quietly congratulating ourselves, or we are desirous of the approval of our divine Father alone.

Whether Pharisees sometimes literally had trumpeters marching before them when they presented their gifts, or whether Jesus was painting an amusing caricature does not really matter. In either case he was rebuking our childish anxiety to be highly esteemed by others.

Hypocrisy is the word which Jesus used to characterize this display. In classical Greek the *hypokritēs* was first an orator and then an actor. So figuratively the word came to be applied to anybody who treats this world as a stage on which to play a part. The religious hypocrite takes some practice which is a real activity and turns it into what it was never meant to be, a piece of make-believe, a theatrical display before an audience. And it is all done for applause.

Of such people Jesus says with emphasis, "They have received their reward in full" (Matthew 6:2). The verb translated "have" was at that time a technical term in commercial transactions; it meant to receive a payment in full and give a receipt. Hypocrites who seek applause will get it, but that is all the reward they will receive.

Having forbidden his followers to give to the needy in the ostentatious manner of the Pharisees, Jesus now tells the Christian way, which is the way of secrecy. The right hand is normally the active hand. Jesus assumes we will use it when we hand over our gift. He adds that our left hand must not be watching. Not only are we not to tell others about our giving; there is a sense in which we are not even to tell ourselves. We are not to be *self-conscious* in our giving, for self-

consciousness will readily deteriorate into self-righteousness.

To sum up, our Christian giving is to be neither before others (waiting for the clapping to begin), nor even before ourselves (our left hand applauding our right hand's generosity) but before God, who sees our secret heart and rewards us with the discovery that, as Jesus said, "It is more blessed to give than to receive" (Acts 20:35).

2. Christian praying. In his second example of the religious kind of righteousness, Jesus depicts two people at prayer. Again the basic difference is between hypocrisy and reality.

What he says of the hypocrites sounds fine at first. They love to pray. But unfortunately it is not prayer which they love, nor the God they are supposed to be praying to. No, they love themselves and the opportunity which public praying gives them to parade themselves.

Of course the discipline of regular prayer is good; all devout Jews prayed three times a day like Daniel (Daniel 6:10). And there was nothing wrong in standing to pray, for this was the usual posture of prayer among Jews. Nor were they necessarily mistaken to pray on the streets as well as in the synagogues. But Jesus uncovered their true motive for praying: "to be seen by others" (Matthew 6:5). Behind their piety lurked their pride.

How then should Christians pray? We are to close the door against disturbance and distraction but also to shut out the prying eyes of others and to shut ourselves in with God. Only then can we obey the Lord's next command: "Pray to your Father, who is unseen" (Matthew 6:6). Our Father is there, waiting to welcome us. Just as nothing destroys prayer like side-glances at human spectators, so nothing enriches it like a sense of the presence of God. For he sees not the outward appearance but only the heart, not the one who is praying only but the motive for which the person prays. As we are to give out of a genuine love for people, so we are to pray out of a genuine love for God.

Our Lord's emphasis on the need for secrecy should not be driven to extremes. If all our praying were to be kept secret, we would have to give up churchgoing, family prayers and prayer meetings. His reference here is to private prayer. The Greek words are in the singular. Jesus has not yet come to public prayer.

3. *Christian fasting.* Matthew 6:16-18 is a passage of Scripture which is commonly ignored. I suspect that some of us live our Christian lives as if these verses had been torn out of our Bibles. Most Christians lay stress on daily prayer and sacrificial giving, but few lay any stress on fasting. In the Sermon on the Mount, Jesus told us how to fast, on the assumption that we would. And in Acts and the New Testament letters there are several references to the apostles fasting. So we cannot dismiss fasting as either an Old Testament practice abrogated in the New Testament or a Catholic practice rejected by Protestants.

Fasting, strictly speaking, is a total abstention from food. It can be legitimately extended, however, to mean going without food partially or totally, for shorter or longer periods. There can be no doubt that in Scripture fasting has to do in various ways with self-denial and self-discipline.

Sometimes fasting was an expression of penitence for past sin. When people were deeply distressed over their sin and guilt, they would both weep and fast. Sometimes still today, when the people of God are convicted of sin and moved to repentance, it is not inappropriate as a token of penitence to mourn, to weep and to fast.

We are to humble ourselves before God not only in penitence for past sin, but also in dependence on him for future mercy. If penitence and fasting go together in Scripture, prayer and fasting are even more often coupled. This is not so much a regular practice, so

that whenever we pray we fast, as an occasional or special arrangement, so that when we need to seek God for some particular direction or blessing we turn aside from food and other distractions in order to do so.

There is another biblical reason for fasting. Hunger is one of our basic human appetites, and greed one of our basic human sins. So self-control is meaningless unless it includes the control of our bodies, and is impossible without self-discipline. Fasting, a voluntary abstinence from food, is one way of increasing our self-control.

One further reason for fasting should be mentioned, namely a deliberate doing without in order to share what we might have eaten (or its cost) with the undernourished. To have an occasional or regular "hungerlunch" or to miss a meal once or twice a week, and at all times to avoid overeating, are forms of fasting which please God because they express a sense of solidarity with the poor.

So whether for penitence or for prayer, for self-discipline or for solidarity, there are good biblical reasons for fasting. Whatever our reasons, Jesus took it for granted that fasting would have a place in our Christian life. His concern was that, as with our giving and praying, we should not draw attention to ourselves.

Looking back over these verses, it is evident that throughout Jesus has been contrasting two alternative kinds of piety, Pharisaic and Christian. Pharisaic piety is ostentatious, motivated by vanity and rewarded by people. Christian piety is secret, motivated by humility and rewarded by God.

Absolute secrecy is impossible for any of us. Even if no human being is there, God is watching us. So the question is: which spectator matters to us more, earthly or heavenly? People or God? We can bluff a human audience, but God is not mocked; we cannot deceive him. God looks on the heart. That is why to do anything in order to be seen by others is bound to degrade it, while to do it to be seen by God is equally bound to ennoble it.

We must choose God for our audience. It is only when we are aware of his presence that our giving, praying and fasting will be real.

What's the main idea in this section?

What is one thing you can act on based on this reading?

PART 4. DISCUSS
Putting It All Together

OPEN

Suppose a friend whom you invite to Bible study declines, saying that all Christians are hypocrites. What evidence is there that this is *not* true of the members of your small group and/or church?

READ MATTHEW 6:1-6, 16-18.

Not conforming to the world is a familiar New Testament concept. What is not so well known is that Jesus also called us not to conform to the religious establishment. He saw (and foresaw) the worldliness of the nominal church and commanded the Christian community to be truly distinct from it in life and practice.

1. In "Connect: Scripture to Scripture," what did you learn about Old Testament law and God's expectations for his people in caring for the poor?

2. From the reading in part three, what are three possible motives for giving?

3. The word *hypocrite* comes from the world of theater. Why is that an appropriate word for Jesus to use here in regard to how we pray?

4. How is our praying to be different from hypocritical praying?

5. In this passage Jesus talks about giving, praying and fasting. Why do you think fasting is less popular than giving and praying?

6. What are some worldly "rewards" of giving for selfish reasons?

7. Have you ever been accused of hypocrisy, and if so, how did you react?

8. What are some ways you have "sounded trumpets," or at least been tempted to, when you have given?

9. Where is the best "room" you have found in which to have undistracted private prayer? Consider various areas, indoors or outdoors.

10. What have been your experiences with fasting?

11. How have you experienced rewards from God for giving, praying and/or fasting?

12. In which of these three areas (perhaps all three!) do you especially want the Holy Spirit to purify your motives?

Pray together (in this case public prayer) that your lives will be free from all forms of hypocrisy.

A Pattern for Dynamic Prayer

Matthew 6:7-15

WHERE WE'RE GOING

The Lord's Prayer was given by Jesus as a model of what genuine Christian prayer should be like. According to Matthew he gave it as a pattern to copy ("This, then, is how you should pray"), and according to Luke he gave it as an actual prayer ("When you pray, say . . ."). We are not obliged to choose, however, for we can both use the prayer as it stands and also model our own praying upon it. Either way, Jesus not only teaches us about prayer but also gives us a greater vision of the God we call "our Father."

Part 1. Investigate: Matthew 6:7-15 (On Your Own)

Part 2. Connect: Scripture to Scripture (On Your Own)

Part 3. Reflect: A Christian's Prayer: *Not Mechanical but Thoughtful* (On Your Own)

Part 4. Discuss: Putting It All Together (With a Group)

A PRAYER TO PRAY

Here's a prayer you can use as you begin to consider genuine Christian prayer:

Our Father in heaven, you are so much greater and higher than we are; yet you allow us to pray to you. In fact, you invite us to bring our needs and requests to you, both physical and spiritual. Help us to always pray according to your will, so that our requests will be pleasing to you. And help us always to remember to thank you for your answers. We ask this in the name of Jesus who taught us how to pray. Amen.

PART 1. INVESTIGATE
Matthew 6:7-15

Read Matthew 6:7-15.

1. What natural divisions do you observe in the Lord's Prayer? What is the focus of each part?

2. How do pagan prayers (v. 7) differ from the persistent prayers Jesus himself offered (Matthew 26:44)?

3. In what ways might we be guilty of mindless, meaningless prayers?

4. If, as Jesus says in verse 8, God already knows what we need, why should Christians pray?

5. What does the phrase "Our Father in heaven" (v. 9) tell us about God?

The image of God as Father is challenging to some in a variety of ways. Scripture gives us God as a good Father. God is not like human fathers, but human fathers are to be like our Father in heaven. If the concept of God as Father is challenging to you, seek to let the truth of who God is transform your mind so you can experience being God's treasured child.

6:7. Jewish scholars were debating the use of fixed prayers in this period; they generally held them to be acceptable if one's intent was genuine. Greek prayers piled up as many titles of the deity addressed as possible, hoping to secure his or her attention. Pagan prayers typically reminded the deity of favors done or sacrifices offered, attempting to get a response from the god on contractual grounds.

6:8. In Judaism, God was a Father who delighted in meeting the needs of his people; Judaism also recognized that God knew all a person's thoughts. Jesus predicates effective prayer on a relationship of intimacy, not a business partnership model, which was closer to the one followed by ancient paganism.

6. What does it mean to "hallow" God's name (v. 9)?

6:9-10. *Jewish people commonly addressed God as "Our heavenly Father" when they prayed, although such intimate titles as "Abba" (Papa) were rare. One standard Jewish prayer of the day (the Kaddish) proclaimed, "Exalted and hallowed be his . . . name . . . and may his kingdom come speedily and soon."*

Jewish prayers recognized that God's name would be "hallowed," or "sanctified," "shown holy," in the time of the end, when his kingdom would come, as the Bible also said (Is 5:16; 29:23; Ezek 36:23; 38:23; 39:7, 27; cf. Zech 14:9). In the present God's people could hallow his name by living rightly; if they lived wrongly, they would "profane" his name, or bring it into disrepute among the nations (cf. also Ex 20:7; Jer 34:16; 44:25-26; Ezek 13:19; 20:14; Amos 2:7). It was understood that after his kingdom came God's will would be done on earth as in heaven.

7. God is already King. In what sense are his kingdom and perfect will still in the future (v. 10)?

8. In our self-centered culture we are often preoccupied with our own little name, empire and will rather than God's. How can we combat this tendency?

9. Some early commentators allegorized the word *bread* (v. 11), assuming that Jesus could not be referring to something as mundane as our physical needs. Why is it perfectly appropriate to pray for actual "daily bread"?

10. How is our heavenly Father's forgiveness related to our forgiving others (vv. 12, 14-15)?

11. If God cannot tempt us and trials are beneficial (James 1:2, 13), then what is the meaning of verse 13?

6:11. *This verse alludes to God's provision of "daily bread" (manna) for his people in the wilderness after he first redeemed them. Prayers for God to supply one's basic needs—of which bread and water are the ultimate examples—were common in the ancient world (cf. Prov 30:8).*

12. In what ways do your prayers need to more closely resemble this model prayer?

Take time now to pray, using the Lord's Prayer as your model.

6:12. *Jewish teaching regarded sins as "debts" before God; the same Aramaic word could be used for both. Biblical law required the periodic forgiveness of monetary debtors (in the seventh and fiftieth years), so the illustration of forgiving debts would have been a graphic one (especially since Jewish lawyers had found a way to circumvent the release of debts so that creditors would continue to lend).*

PART 2. CONNECT
Scripture to Scripture

THE VITAL FAMILY CONNECTION: ISRAEL AS GOD'S CHILD

Anyone who prays the Lord's Prayer begins by addressing God as "our Father." Everything in the prayer flows from our initial ability to call God *Father.* It is the certainty of this vital family connection that enables us to pray the rest of the Lord's Prayer.

The New Testament idea of God as Father is well known. Less known is the fact that the concept of God as Father is already present in the Old Testament.

When the Israelites were enslaved in Egypt, the Lord sent Moses to confront the Egyptian Pharaoh and demand that he free the Israelites. Read Exodus 4:21-23. How does the Lord tell Moses to identify Israel to Pharaoh?

_____

_____

_____

_____

This family relationship between God and Israel continued throughout their forty years of wandering. When Israel was about to enter Canaan at last, Moses reviewed for the people the entire history of their exodus from Egypt.

Read Deuteronomy 8:1-5, which recalls the Lord's faithful provision during the Israelites' desert travels, despite their complaints and rebellion. Fill in the missing parts of verse 5:

"Know then _____ that as _____,

so the LORD your God _____."

The Lord warned Moses that after Israel was successfully established in Canaan, they would grow self-satisfied and would rebel against him yet again. In preparation for that time, he instructed Moses to write down a song and teach it to the Israelites; the remembered song would testify against them in the time of their rebellion. This song is recorded in Deuteronomy 32.

Read Deuteronomy 32:1-6. According to verse 6, what made Israel's rebellion especially contemptible?

_____

_____

_____

_____

Centuries later, during a time of flagrant idolatry, the prophet Hosea tried to call Israel back to God. The book of Hosea alternates between terrifying images of judgment and tender words of hope and mercy. In Hosea 11, the Lord recalls the exodus from Egypt. Read Hosea 11:1-4 and write out verse 1, noting the strong relationship that God claims with Israel.

_____

_____

_____

_____

LIKE A FATHER

Besides identifying God as Father, a number of places in the Old Testament express the Lord's character as being *like* a father in various ways. We have already looked at one of these references in Deuteronomy 8:5. Read the following additional Scriptures and match up what they say about how God acts as a father.

Deuteronomy 1:29-31	He has compassion on his children.
Psalm 103:13-14	He disciplines his children.
Proverbs 3:11-12	He carries his children.

APPEALING TO THE FATHER

The Old Testament prophets were not afraid to hold God accountable for his fatherhood of Israel and to demand that God act as Father for his people.

Read Isaiah 63:15–64:12, part of a heartfelt plea from the time of the exile to Babylon. What does the writer appeal to God to do because he is Father? Note especially 63:16 and 64:8.

_____

_____

_____

_____

CALLING GOD "FATHER" DOES NOT EQUAL OBEDIENCE

Through the prophet Jeremiah, the Lord expressed his desire that his people would acknowledge him as Father. Yet he made it clear that using the word *Father* was not enough.

Read Jeremiah 3, noting especially verses 4-5 and 19-20.

How had the people been insincere in calling God "my Father"?

____ a. They were always angry.

____ b. Their words did not match their deeds.

____ c. They did not worship at the prescribed times.

____ d. They had lost the Ark of the Covenant.

____ e. They felt doubts.

What was God's intention and hope for the people of Judah?

____ a. That they would follow the northern kingdom of Israel into exile

____ b. That they would call him "Father" and not some other name

____ c. That they would explore new lands in his name

____ d. That they would call him "Father" and remain faithful to him

____ e. That they would make another Ark of the Covenant

UNBREAKABLE FATHERHOOD

Despite Judah's rebellion and the fact that they would be taken into exile in Babylon, the Lord held on to his purposes for them and kept his commitment to them. He promised to lead them back home from exile, and he explained why. Read Jeremiah 31:7-9. Ephraim was the younger son of Joseph (Genesis 41:50-52); as the ancestor of Jeroboam, first king of the northern kingdom of Israel (1 Kings 10:26), Ephraim's name became synonymous with Israel. Write out the last part of Jeremiah 31:9, beginning with the word *because*:

_____

_____

_____

_____

_____

OTHER SCRIPTURAL FORETASTES OF THE LORD'S PRAYER

The God we call "Father" in the Lord's Prayer is the same unchanging God who has always listened to the prayers of his people. In the Old Testament we can find forerunners of the petitions in the Lord's Prayer.

Read the following Scriptures. Identify the plea in the Lord's Prayer which each one echoes.

Proverbs 30:7-9   "_____"

Exodus 16:13-19   "_____"

Ezekiel 36:23   "_____"

The faithfulness of God gave Old Testament people the courage to pray for what they needed, and to trust God to provide even when they did not understand what they needed. The faithfulness of God found perfect expression in his Son, who taught us and still teaches us how to pray to our Father.

PART 3. REFLECT
A Christian's Prayer
NOT MECHANICAL BUT THOUGHTFUL

Hypocrisy is not the only sin to avoid in prayer; "babbling like pagans" (Matthew 6:7), or meaningless, mechanical utterance, is another. The former is the folly of the Pharisee, the latter of the Gentile or pagan. Hypocrisy is the misuse of the *purpose* of prayer (diverting it from the glory of God to the glory of self); verbosity is a misuse of the very *nature* of prayer (degrading it from a real and personal approach to God into a mere recitation of words).

We see again that the method of Jesus is to paint a vivid contrast between two alternatives in order to indicate his way the more plainly. Regarding the practice of prayer, he contrasts the pagan way of meaningless loquacity with the Christian way of meaningful communion with God. Thus Jesus is always calling his followers to something higher than the attainments of those around them, whether religious people or secular people.

"Do not keep on babbling like pagans," he says. The Greek verb *battalogeō* is unique not only in biblical literature but elsewhere as well; no other use of the word is known beyond quotations of this verse. Most regard it as an onomatopoeic expression, the sound of the word indicating its meaning. The word describes any and every prayer which is all words and no meaning, all lips and no mind and heart. "For they think they will be heard because of their many words." What an incredible notion! What sort of a God is this who is chiefly impressed by the mechanics and the statistics of prayer, and whose response is determined by the volume of words we use and the number of hours we spend in praying? Christians do not believe in that kind of God. On the contrary, "your Father knows what you need before you ask him." He is our Father—a Father who loves his chil-

dren and knows all about their needs.

If the praying of Pharisees was hypocritical and that of pagans mechanical, then the praying of Christians must be real—sincere as opposed to hypocritical, thoughtful as opposed to mechanical. Jesus intends our minds and hearts to be involved in what we are saying. Then prayer is seen in its true light, not as meaningless repetition of words, nor as a means to our own glorification, but as a true communion with our heavenly Father. He is personal; he is loving; he is powerful. He is not only good but great. God combines fatherly love with heavenly power, and what his love directs his power is able to perform.

In telling us to address God as "our Father in heaven," the concern of Jesus is not with protocol (teaching us the correct etiquette in approaching the Deity) but with truth (that we may come to him in the right frame of mind). Then the content of our prayers will be radically affected in two ways. First, God's concerns will be given priority ("your name . . . your kingdom . . . your will"). Second, our own needs, though demoted to second place, will yet be comprehensively committed to him ("Give us . . . forgive us . . . deliver us").

The first three petitions in the Lord's Prayer express our concern for God's glory in relation to his name, rule and will. If our concept of God were of some impersonal force, then of course he would have no personal name, rule or will to be concerned about. But if he is in reality "our Father in heaven," the personal God of love and power fully revealed by Jesus Christ, Creator of all, who cares about the creatures he has made and the children he has redeemed, then and then only does it become possible (indeed, essential) to give his concerns priority and to become preoccupied with his name, his kingdom and his will.

The name of God is not a combination of the letters *G, O* and *D.* The *name* stands for the person who bears it, for his character and activity. So God's *name* is God himself as he is in himself and has revealed himself. His name is already "holy" in that it is separate from and exalted over every other name. But we pray that it may be *hallowed,* treated as holy, because we ardently desire that due honor may be given to it, that is to him whose name it is, in our own lives, in the church and in the world.

The kingdom of God is his royal rule. He is already King, reigning in absolute sovereignty over both nature and history. Yet when Jesus came he announced a new and special break-in of the kingly rule of God, with all the blessings of salvation and the demands of submission which the divine rule implies. To pray that his kingdom may "come" is to pray both that it may grow, as through the church's witness people submit to Jesus, and that soon it will be consummated when Jesus returns in glory to take his power and reign.

The will of God is "good, pleasing and perfect" (Romans 12:2), for it is the will of "our Father in heaven" who is infinite in knowledge, love and power. As his name is already holy and he is already King, so already his will is being done "in heaven." What Jesus bids us pray is that life on earth may come to approximate more nearly to life in heaven.

It is comparatively easy to repeat the words of the Lord's Prayer like a parrot or indeed like a pagan "babbler." To pray them with sincerity, however, has revolutionary implications, for it expresses the priorities of a Christian. In the Christian counterculture our top priority is not our own name, kingdom and will, but God's. Whether we can pray these petitions with integrity is a searching test of the reality and depth of our Christian profession.

In the second half of the Lord's Prayer the possessive adjective changes from *your* to *our* as we turn from God's affairs to our own. Having expressed our burning concern for his glory, we now express our humble dependence on his grace. To decline to mention our concerns at all in prayer is as great an error as to allow them to dominate our prayers. Since God is our Father in heaven and loves us with a father's love, he is concerned for the total welfare of his children and wants us to bring our needs trustingly to him, our need of food and of forgiveness and of deliverance from evil.

Some early commentators could not believe that Jesus intended our first request to be for literal bread for the body. We should be thankful for the greater, down-to-earth, biblical understanding of the Reformers. The petition that God will "give" us our food does not deny that most people have to earn their own living, that farmers have to plow, sow and reap, and that we are commanded to feed the hungry ourselves. Instead, it is an expression of ultimate dependence on God who normally uses human means of production and distribution through which to fulfill his purposes. Moreover, it seems that Jesus wanted his followers to be conscious of a day-to-day dependence.

Forgiveness is as indispensable to the life and health of the soul as food is to the body. So the next prayer is "Forgive us our debts." Sin is likened to a debt because it deserves to be punished. But when God forgives sin, he remits the penalty and drops the charge against us. The addition of the words "as we also have forgiven our debtors" is further emphasized in verses 14 and 15 which follow the prayer and state that our Father will forgive us if we forgive others but will not forgive us if we refuse to forgive others. This certainly does not mean that our forgiveness of others earns us the right to be forgiven. It is rather that God forgives only the penitent and that one of the chief evidences of true penitence is a forgiving spirit.

The last two petitions should probably be

understood as the negative and positive aspects of one: "Lead us not into temptation, but deliver us from the evil one." The sinner whose evil in the past has been forgiven longs to be delivered from its tyranny in the future. But two problems confront us. First, the Bible says that God does not (indeed cannot) tempt us with evil (James 1:13). So what is the sense of praying that he will not do what he has promised never to do? I believe "lead us not" must be understood in the light of its counterpart "but deliver us" and that "evil" is correctly rendered "the evil one." It is the devil who is in view, who tempts God's people to sin, and from whom we need to be rescued.

The second problem concerns the fact that the Bible says temptation and trial are good for us (James 1:2). The probable answer is that the prayer is more that we may overcome temptation than that we may avoid it. Perhaps we could paraphrase the whole request as "Do not allow us so to be led into temptation that it overwhelms us, but rescue us from the evil one."

Thus the three petitions which Jesus puts upon our lips are beautifully comprehensive. They cover, in principle, all our human need—material (daily bread), spiritual (forgiveness of sins) and moral (deliverance from evil). What we are doing whenever we pray this prayer is to express our dependence on God in every area of our human life.

Jesus seems to have given the Lord's Prayer as a model of *real* prayer, *Christian* prayer, in distinction to the prayers of Pharisees and pagans. To be sure, one could recite the Lord's Prayer either hypocritically or mechanically or both. But if we mean what we say, then the Lord's Prayer is the divine alternative to both forms of false prayer.

Christian prayer is *God-centered* (concerned for God's glory) in contrast to the self-centeredness of the Pharisees (preoccupied with their own glory). And it is *intelligent* (expressive of thoughtful dependence) in contrast to the mechanical incantations of the pagans. The tragic mistake of Pharisees and pagans, of hypocrite and heathen, is to be found in their false image of God. Neither is really thinking of God at all, for the hypocrite thinks only of self while the heathen thinks of other things. If we allow Scripture to fashion our image of God, if we recall his character and practice his presence, we shall never pray with hypocrisy but always with integrity, never mechanically but always thoughtfully, like the children of God that we are.

What's the main idea in this section?

What is one thing you can act on based on this reading?

PART 4. DISCUSS
Putting It All Together

OPEN

Imagine that your prayers, like those in the Psalms, were recorded for others to read. What would people learn about your image of God?

READ MATTHEW 6:7-15.

The fundamental difference between various kinds of prayer is the fundamentally different images of God that lie behind them.

1. How should our attitude in prayer keep us from praying like the pagans (vv. 7-8)?

2. What natural divisions did you observe in the Lord's Prayer?

3. What did you see as the focus of each division?

4. What did you learn in "Connect: Scripture to Scripture" about the concept of the fatherhood of God expressed in the Old Testament?

5. What does it mean to honor the name of God?

6. How does unforgiveness cause problems in our prayer life (vv. 14-15)?

7. What are you pleased or encouraged about regarding your prayer life?

8. What area(s) of prayer do you struggle with?

9. When you pray the Lord's Prayer in church, it's likely that you sometimes say the words automatically, and other times you really think about the words. What makes the difference?

10. How aware are you that you must depend on your Father in heaven for your *daily* food?

11. When have you seen the Lord deliver you from temptation?

12. How seriously do you take Matthew 6:14-15 concerning forgiveness?

Close by praying the Lord's Prayer together, slowly, paying close attention to the words and meaning them from your hearts.

SESSION NINE

What God Thinks
of My Ambitions

Matthew 6:19-34

WHERE WE'RE GOING

Everyone is ambitious to be or to do something. Childhood ambitions tend to follow certain stereotypes—to be an athlete, astronaut or movie star. Adults have their own narrow stereotypes too—to be wealthy, famous or powerful. But ultimately there are only two possible ambitions for human beings. Will Christian faith make a difference as you set your ambitions? In this passage Jesus points out the folly of the wrong way and the wisdom of the right. Then he invites us to compare them and decide for ourselves.

> Part 1. Investigate: Matthew 6:19-34 (On Your Own)
>
> Part 2. Connect: Scripture to Scripture (On Your Own)
>
> Part 3. Reflect: A Christian's Ambition: *Not Material Security but God's Rule* (On Your Own)
>
> Part 4. Discuss: Putting It All Together (With a Group)

A PRAYER TO PRAY

Here's a prayer you can use as you continue to think about genuine Christian prayer:

God of peace, giver of every good and perfect gift, we should be living in a way that reflects your peace. But we are such worriers. We waste time and energy trying to control our destinies, when we should be putting our lives into your hands. Give us single-mindedness to serve only you. Give us trust and confidence that you are taking care of all our needs. Give us peace so that others will see your peace and be attracted to you. We pray this in the name of Jesus, the Prince of Peace. Amen.

PART 1. INVESTIGATE
Matthew 6:19-34

Read Matthew 6:19-34.

1. What, according to Jesus, are the most important things in life?

6:19. *Ancient teachers like Hillel, a famous Jewish teacher, generally acknowledged the corruptibility of earthly treasure. Because thieves could dig through walls and steal a strongbox in one's home, well-to-do people usually tried one of several other methods to safeguard their wealth: investing money with moneychangers, depositing it in a temple for safekeeping (even most robbers balked at "robbing gods") or burying it in the ground or in caves, where, however, moth (for expensive apparel) or rust (for coins) could destroy its value in time.*

2. Why should we store up heavenly treasures rather than earthly ones (vv. 19-21)?

Does this mean that we cannot have personal property, savings accounts or insurance policies? Explain.

3. Practically speaking, how can we store up treasure in heaven?

6:22-23. *Jesus speaks literally of a "single" [NIV "healthy"] eye versus a "bad" or "evil" [NIV "unhealthy"] one. This saying may involve several plays on words. A "single" eye normally meant a generous one but also sets the reader up for 6:24. A "bad" eye in that culture could mean either a diseased one or a stingy one. Many people believed that light was emitted from the eye, enabling one to see, rather than that light was admitted*

4. How are physical and spiritual sight (or blindness) similar (vv. 22-23)?

5. Many people hold two jobs and are able to satisfy two bosses. So why would Jesus say that it is impossible to serve two masters—God and money (v. 24)?

6. How will the crucial choices we make in verses 19-24 affect our ability to live free from worry (v. 25)?

7. According to Jesus, why are we foolish to worry about our physical and material needs (vv. 25-30)?

through the eye. Although here Jesus compares the eye to a lamp, he speaks of "diseased" [NIV "unhealthy"] eyes which fail to admit light. Such eyes become a symbol for the worthlessness of a stingy person.

8. How does worry also reveal a lack of faith (v. 30)?

9. If God promises to feed and clothe his children, then why are many of them ill-clad and undernourished (see Matthew 25:41-45)?

6:25. *Most people in antiquity had little beyond basic necessities—food, clothing and shelter. Because their acquisition of these necessities often depended—especially in rural areas—on seasonal rains or (in Egypt) the flooding of the Nile, they had plenty of cause for stress even about food and clothing.*

10. Give examples of how people today "run after all these things" that Jesus mentions (v. 32).

11. Why and how are our ambitions to be different from those of non-Christians (vv. 32-34)?

12. How has this passage challenged you to reexamine your goals and ambitions?

6:28-30. *Some commentators have suggested that the flowers here may be anemones, which were purple, the color that many ancient readers would have envisioned for Solomon's royal robes (6:29). Yet such flowers were fuel for the oven. The perishing of grass and flowers as they dried up in each year's summer heat was a natural image for human mortality.*

In prayer, talk with God over the issue of commitment. Will you hand over your priorities to him?

PART 2. CONNECT
Scripture to Scripture

EARTHLY TREASURES

The Old Testament takes an evenhanded view of earthly wealth. On the one hand, material riches are a blessing from God and a cause for thankfulness. On the other hand, people should not make wealth their chief aim, and they should always be aware that earthly wealth is transient.

Read Proverbs 23:4-5 for a graphic description of what happens to earthly wealth. What is the emphasis in this passage?

_____

_____

_____

_____

Sketch a picture that illustrates the description of how riches can suddenly depart.

What are some ways that riches "fly off to the sky"?

_____

_____

_____

_____

The writer of Ecclesiastes, another book of wisdom like Proverbs, is often given to extreme statements, yet he does offer a balanced view of wealth. Read Ecclesiastes 5:10-20. For each of the multiple-choice questions below, check all the statements which are true strictly according to *this* passage:

Wealth can become a burden because

____ a. anxiety over keeping it causes sleeplessness.

____ b. it causes overindulgence.

____ c. no one gives you credit for all your hard work to earn it.

____ d. it causes dissatisfaction.

____ e. it can be easily lost.

Wealth can be a blessing when

___ a. it enables you to help others.

___ b. it is accompanied by happiness in your work.

___ c. it is gotten by inheritance.

___ d. God enables you to have the time to enjoy it.

___ e. you are able to pass it along to your heirs.

What significance does the writer of Ecclesiastes see in the fact that we all come into the world and leave it "naked" (vv. 15-16)?

_____

_____

_____

_____

What advice does Psalm 62:10 give for a person to whom God grants wealth? Write out the second half of the verse word-for-word:

_____

_____

_____

_____

The verse you have just written—a verse Jesus' hearers most likely would have recognized—tells us where *not* to set our hearts. Now we turn to where the Old Testament Scriptures tell us we *should* set our hearts.

ONLY ONE MASTER

In our culture the concept of having only one master is hard to grasp. A person today could work two (or more!) jobs and have several employers who compete for their time, energy and loyalty. But the idea was well known in Old Testament times as well as in Jesus' time. A slave has only one owner and therefore only one master.

Throughout their history, the Israelites often forgot their position as slaves of the one true God—their good, loving Master God. They thought they could serve him *and* the idols of surrounding nations. For example, under King Ahab and Queen Jezebel, Israel fell into worship of the fertility god Baal. The prophet Elijah boldly confronted Ahab and demanded a showdown with the prophets of Baal.

Read 1 Kings 18:16-39. Verse 21 includes a question and a statement.

Fill in the missing parts of Elijah's question:

"How long will _____ between _____?"

Fill in the missing parts of Elijah's statement:

"If _____, follow him; but if Baal is God,

_____."

What contrast did the people witness between Baal and the Lord, leading to their declaration in verse 39?

_____

_____

_____

_____

Read Judges 2:8-19. What contrast do you find between the times when Israel chose to follow false gods (the Baals) and when they chose to follow the Lord?

_____

_____

_____

_____

What insight does this passage offer into Jesus' words in Matthew 6:24 about serving two masters?

_____

_____

_____

_____

WORRY

"Do not worry about your life," Jesus said (Matthew 6:25). Essentially, he was saying, "Don't put all your energy into getting what you want." David said something very similar in Psalm 37, not once but repeatedly. Read Psalm 37 and note the numbers of all the verses which refer to fretting or worrying:

Verse numbers:_____

What, specifically, is David instructing the Israelites not to worry about?

_____

_____

_____

What reasons does Psalm 37 give that the Lord's people should *not* worry?

_____

_____

_____

_____

David, the writer of Psalm 37, knew he was God's chosen replacement for King Saul. David could have been consumed with getting what was rightfully his—the throne. He could even have felt righteous about his obsession. Instead, he held back, pursuing God's kingdom and righteousness, refusing to press his advantage when circumstances seemed to hand him the kingdom.

Read 1 Samuel 24. Here David had the perfect opportunity to do away with Saul and assume the kingship. What reasons did David give for sparing Saul's life?

_____

_____

_____

_____

What connections do you see between David's confidence in God expressed in Psalm 37 and his words and actions in 1 Samuel 24?

_____

_____

_____

_____

THE GRASS OF THE FIELD

In his sermon Jesus asks his hearers why they worry about clothing. The humble plants of the fields, he said, are clothed more lavishly than King Solomon, even though they are destined to be burned up (Matthew 6:28-30).

To get an idea of just how lavishly King Solomon was clothed, read 1 Kings 10:14-29. Although Solomon's clothing is not mentioned, the chapter details much of his wealth. What items of his were made out of gold?

_____

_____

_____

_____

Based on the description you have just read, what do you think Solomon's clothing looked like?

_____

_____

_____

_____

Jesus said that God clothes the lilies and grass of the field in "clothing" more beautiful than Solomon's. In the Old Testament, grass serves as a symbol of God's generous provision but also as a symbol of the transitory nature of human life.

Return to Psalm 37. What comparison is drawn in verse 2?

_____

_____

_____

_____

Now read Isaiah 40:6-8. What contrast is drawn between grass and the word of God?

_____

_____

_____

_____

Scholars note, "Grass in shallow soil, subject to the vagaries of drought and rain, is a changeable phenomenon, quickly green when it has moisture and just as quickly brown when it lacks water. In such a climate even the morning dew can renew grass (Ps 90:5). Another factor is the grass that grows on housetops. Seeds inevitably sprout on the roofs of mud houses, but soon after appearing with the rain they wither, for their roots are shallow, and they cannot endure the sun and winds (2 Kings 19:26; Ps 129:6; Is 37:27)."[1]

Based on all you have read in this section, as well as Matthew 6:19-34, on what kinds of things does Jesus *want* us to spend our time and energy?

_____

_____

_____

_____

---

[1]Leland Ryken, James C. Wilhoit and Tremper Longman, eds., "Grass," in *Dictionary of Biblical Imagery* (Downers Grove, IL: InterVarsity Press, 1998), p. 349.

PART 3. REFLECT
A Christian's Ambition
NOT MATERIAL SECURITY BUT GOD'S RULE

In the first half of Matthew 6 (vv. 1-18) Jesus describes the Christian's *private* life (giving, praying, fasting); in the second half (vv. 19-34) he is concerned with our *public* business in the world (questions of money, possessions, food, drink, clothing and ambition). In both spheres the same insistent summons of Jesus is heard, the call to be different from the popular culture: different from the hypocrisy of the religious (vv. 1-18) and now different also from the materialism of the irreligious (vv. 19-34).

Jesus places the alternatives before us at every stage. There are two treasures (on earth and in heaven), two bodily conditions (light and darkness), two masters (God and money) and two preoccupations (our bodies and God's kingdom). We cannot sit on the fence. Jesus sets the false and the true over against each other in such a way as to invite us to compare them and see for ourselves.

In verses 19-21, the point to which Jesus directs our attention is *the comparative durability of the two treasures*. It ought to be easy to decide which to collect, because *treasures on earth* are corruptible and therefore insecure, while *treasures in heaven* are incorruptible and therefore secure. If our object is to lay up treasure, we shall presumably concentrate on the kind which will last and can be stored without either depreciation or deterioration.

What Jesus forbids his followers is the selfish accumulation of goods, extravagant and luxurious living, the hardheartedness which does not feel the colossal need of the world's underprivileged people, the foolish fantasy that a person's life consists in the abundance of possessions, and the materialism which tethers our hearts to the earth. For the Sermon on the Mount repeatedly refers to the *heart,* and here Jesus declares that our heart always follows our treasure, whether down to earth or up to heaven.

Nothing was safe in the ancient world. Moths got into people's clothes, rats and mice ate the stored grain, worms took whatever was put underground, and thieves broke into their homes and stole what they kept there. For us moderns, who try to protect our treasure by insecticides, rat poison, mousetraps, rustproof paints and burglar alarms, it disintegrates instead through inflation or devaluation or an economic slump. Even if some of it lasts through this life, we can take none of it with us to the next.

But "treasures in heaven" are incorruptible. What are they? Jesus does not explain. Yet surely we may say that to "store up treasures in heaven" is to do anything on earth whose effects last for eternity. It seems to refer to such things as the development of Christian character; the increase of faith, hope and love; growth in the knowledge of Christ whom one day we shall see face to face; the active endeavor (by prayer and witness) to introduce others to Christ; and the use of our money for Christian causes. All these are temporal activities with eternal consequences. No burglar can steal them, and no vermin can destroy them. So treasures in heaven are secure.

Jesus turns from the comparative durability of the two treasures to the comparative benefit to be derived from two conditions. The contrast is between a blind person and a sighted person and so between the light and darkness in which they respectively live. While blind people often cope wonderfully, the principle holds that a sighted person walks in the light, while a blind person is in darkness. Not infrequently in Scripture the *eye* is equivalent to the *heart*. That is, to "set the heart" and to "fix the eye" on something are synonyms. Just as our eye affects our whole body, so our ambition (where we fix our eyes and heart) affects our whole life.

It is all a question of vision. If we have spiritual vision, if our spiritual perspective is correctly adjusted, then our life is filled with purpose and drive. But if our vision becomes clouded by the false god of materialism and we lose our sense of values, then our whole life is in darkness and we cannot see where we are going.

Jesus now explains that behind the choice between two treasures (where we lay them up) and two visions (where we fix our eyes) there lies the still more basic choice between two masters (whom we are going to serve). It is a choice between God and mammon, that is, between the living Creator himself and any object of our own creation we term "money" (*mammon* being the transliteration of an Aramaic word for wealth). For we cannot serve both.

Anybody who divides allegiance between God and mammon has already given it to mammon, since God can be served only with an entire and exclusive devotion. To try to share him with other loyalties is to have opted for idolatry. Now it is a question not just of comparative durability and comparative benefit, but of comparative worth: the intrinsic worth of the One and the intrinsic worthlessness of the other.

It is a pity that Matthew 6:25-34 is often read on its own in church, isolated from what has gone before. Then the significance of the introductory "Therefore I tell you" is missed. So we must begin by relating this "therefore," this conclusion of Jesus, to the teaching which has led up to it. He calls us to thought before he calls us to action. He invites us to look clearly and coolly at the alternatives before us and to weigh them carefully. Only when we have grasped the comparative durability of the two treasures (corruptible and incorruptible),

the comparative usefulness of the two eye conditions (light and darkness) and the comparative worth of the two masters (God and mammon) are we ready to make our choice. And only when we have made our choice—for heavenly treasure, for light, for God— "therefore I tell you" this is how you must go on and behave.

Christ's language of *searching,* contrasting what the Gentiles seek with what his followers are to seek first, introduces us to the subject of ambition. Jesus took it for granted that all human beings are seekers. It is not natural for people to drift aimlessly through life like plankton. Our Lord simplifies the issue for us by reducing the alternative possible life goals to only two. He puts them over against each other in this section, urging his followers not to be preoccupied with their own security but rather with God's rule and God's righteousness and with their spread and triumph in the world.

Most of verses 25-34 are negative. Jesus forbids us to be preoccupied with food, drink and clothing. Now Jesus Christ neither denies nor despises the needs of the body. As a matter of fact, he made it and he takes care of it. He is emphasizing that to become engrossed in material comforts is a false preoccupation. For one thing it is unproductive; for another it is unnecessary; but especially it is unworthy. It betrays a false view of human beings (as if they were only bodies needing to be fed, watered, clothed and housed) and of human life (as if it were merely a psychological mechanism needing to be protected, lubricated and fueled). Is physical well-being a worthy object to which to devote our lives? Has human life no more significance than this? For you my disciples, Jesus implies, they are a hopelessly unworthy goal. They are not the supreme good in life.

It is important to see verses 31-33 together. Verse 31 repeats the prohibition against being anxious about food, drink and clothing. Verse 32 adds that the Gentiles seek all these things.

This shows that in the vocabulary of Jesus "to seek" and "to be anxious" are interchangeable. He is not talking so much about anxiety as about ambition. Heathen ambition focuses on material necessities. This cannot be right for Christians partly because *your heavenly Father knows that you need them* but mostly because these things are not an appropriate or worthy object for the Christian's quest. This is no more than an elaboration of teaching already implicit in the Lord's Prayer. We cannot pray the Lord's Prayer until our ambitions have been purified.

When Jesus spoke of the kingdom of God, he was not referring to the general sovereignty of God over nature and history, but to that specific rule over his own people which he himself had inaugurated and which begins in anybody's life when the person humbles himself or herself, repents, believes, submits and is born again. To seek first this kingdom is to desire as of first importance the spread of the reign of Jesus Christ.

It is not clear why Jesus distinguished between "his kingdom" and "his righteousness" as twin but separate objects of our Christian quest. Let me make a tentative suggestion about the difference between the two. God's *kingdom* exists only where Jesus Christ is consciously acknowledged. But God's *righteousness* is (arguably at least) a wider concept. It includes that individual and social righteousness to which reference has been made earlier in the sermon. And God, because he is himself a righteous God, desires righteousness in every human community, not just in every Christian community. Some degree of righteousness is possible in unregenerate society—in personal life, in family standards and in public decency.

To seek first God's kingdom and his righteousness may be said to embrace our Christian evangelistic and social responsibilities, much as do the salt and light metaphors of Matthew 5. In order to seek first God's kingdom we must evangelize, since the kingdom spreads only as the gospel of Christ is preached, heard, believed and obeyed. In order to seek first God's righteousness we shall still evangelize (for the inward righteousness of the heart is impossible otherwise), but we shall also engage in social action and endeavor to spread throughout the community those higher standards of righteousness which are pleasing to God.

What's the main idea in this section?

What is one thing you can act on based on this reading?

PART 4. DISCUSS
Putting It All Together

OPEN

What power has materialism held over you? How hard has it been to break?

READ MATTHEW 6:19-34.

If we are Christians, everything we do, however "secular" it may seem, is "religious" in the sense that it is done in God's presence and according to God's will. One of the emphases Jesus makes in this chapter is that God is equally concerned with both areas of our life—private and public, religious and secular.

1. It's easy to come up with examples of treasures on earth. What are some examples of treasures in heaven?

2. What does it mean to have spiritual vision?

3. Why do you think people try to serve both God and money simultaneously?

4. Despite our efforts to do so, why is it impossible to serve both God and money?

5. Why do verses 25-34 begin with the word "Therefore"?

6. What is the difference between planning for the future and worrying about the future?

7. In what areas of life do you "waver between two opinions" (1 Kings 18:21)? That is, what competes with the Lord for your loyalty and devotion?

8. What does most of your time, energy or money go toward?

9. In what areas has the Lord helped you to spend less time and energy worrying?

10. How does nature help you to understand the Lord's care and provision and perhaps shift your focus or energy?

11. What is one thing in your life that would visibly change if you more diligently pursued God's kingdom and his righteousness?

Reread Matthew 6:34. Then pray, giving your tomorrow to your heavenly Father.

RELATIONSHIPS THAT ENCOURAGE

Matthew 7:1-12

WHERE WE'RE GOING

Matthew 7 may at first appear to be a series of self-contained paragraphs, but there is a connecting thread—relationships. The Christian counterculture is not an individualistic but a community affair, and relations both within the community and between the community and others are of paramount importance.

> **Part 1. Investigate: Matthew 7:1-12 (On Your Own)**
>
> **Part 2. Connect: Scripture to Scripture (On Your Own)**
>
> **Part 3. Reflect: A Christian's Relationships:** *To Our Brothers and Sisters and to Our Father* **(On Your Own)**
>
> **Part 4. Discuss: Putting It All Together (With a Group)**

A PRAYER TO PRAY

Here's a prayer you can use to set you on your way:

Judge of all the earth, only you know what is in people's hearts, and only you are righteous and holy. Therefore only you have the right to judge. Forgive us for being so quick to play God and stand in judgment of others; we should really be looking at our own faults and sins. You have invited us to come to you with our requests, so we pray that you will keep us aware of our need for your mercy. Keep us also grateful for your good gifts, both spiritual and material, so that we will not fall back into self-sufficiency and self-righteousness. We ask this in the name of Jesus. Amen.

PART 1. INVESTIGATE
Matthew 7:1-12

Read Matthew 7:1-12.

7:1-2. *The idea of a measuring scale (the image is from the ancient marketplace) was used elsewhere for the day of judgment or divine retribution; "as a man measures it will be measured back to him" occurs a number of times in later Jewish sources and may have been a maxim. For the principle, see Matthew 5:7, 6:14-15 and Proverbs 19:17. Compare also the Old Testament principles that false witnesses were to receive the penalty they sought for the accused (Deut 19:18-21) and that God opposed unjust judges (Ex 23:6-8; Deut 16:18-20).*

1. What commands does Jesus make in these verses?

2. Why does Jesus tell us not to judge others (vv. 1-2)? How do these verses expand on Jesus' statement about the merciful (5:7)?

3. According to Jesus, why are we often unfit to be judges (vv. 3-4)?

4. Some have assumed that Jesus was forbidding all judgment, even in law courts. How would you respond to this suggestion?

7:6. *Pigs and dogs were considered unclean animals (Prov 26:11; 2 Pet 2:22), which had no appreciation for valuable things (Prov 11:22). Pigs typically ate the vilest foods, and dogs were scavengers, consuming even human blood. Stray dogs were known to growl at those who tossed them food as well as those who ignored them. The image would thus be forceful and beyond*

5. What steps must we take to truly help a brother or sister (v. 5)?

6. What kinds of people do you think Jesus refers to as "dogs" and "pigs" (v. 6)?

7. Why is it futile, even dangerous, to expect such people to value the gospel?

8. What encouragement does Jesus give those who ask, seek and knock (vv. 7-8)?

How can we be assured of these promises (vv. 9-11)?

9. The Jewish Talmud states, "What is hateful to you, do not do to anyone else." Likewise, Confucius told his followers, "Do not to others what you would not wish done to you." How does the golden rule (v. 12) go beyond these commands? In what sense does this rule sum up the Law and the Prophets?

10. Think of a relationship that is presently strained or broken. How would the "rule of love" apply to that relationship?

11. What steps do you want to take this week to help mend that relationship?

Pray that in your relationships with other people you will grow as an encourager.

dispute for ancient hearers. The question is what the verse means in the context. Perhaps it means not correcting (cf. Mt 7:1-5) those who would not listen (cf. Prov 23:9). Perhaps it means giving only to those who want what one offers, as God does (Mt 7:7-11); in this case the text returns to the idea of giving and of reciprocity in verse 12.

7:7-8. *The boldness with which verses 7-8 promise answers to prayer is quite rare in ancient literature.*

7:9-11. *In verses 9-11 Jesus adapts a standard Jewish argument here called* qal vahomer: *arguing from the lesser to the greater (if the lesser is true, how much more the greater). Fish and bread were basic staples, integral to the diet of most of Jesus' hearers; they do not stand for the fineries of the wealthy.*

PART 2. CONNECT
Scripture to Scripture

GLOATING AND BOASTING IN THE DAY OF TROUBLE

> Remember, LORD, what the Edomites did
>   on the day Jerusalem fell.
> "Tear it down," they cried,
>   "tear it down to its foundations!" (Psalm 137:7)

The memory must have been terrible to the exiled Judeans. When the Babylonians destroyed Jerusalem in 587 B.C., Judah's neighbor Edom watched and cheered the Babylonians on. The two nations' rivalry went back to the rivalry between twin brothers Jacob and Esau. Now Esau's descendants—Edom—were gloating over the misfortune of Jacob's descendants. *They had it coming,* Edom's behavior said loud and clear.

Jesus' warning of Matthew 7:1—"Do not judge, or you too will be judged"—was already valid in Old Testament times. Edom had lorded it over Israel and now would be judged for their judgmental spirit. During the exile to Babylon, through the prophet Ezekiel, the Lord had strong words for Edom.

Read Ezekiel 35:1–36:5. Fill in the missing parts of Ezekiel 35:15.

"Because _____when _____

_____, that is how I will treat you. You _____, Mount

Seir, you and all of Edom. Then they will know that _____"

God spoke about Edom through the prophet Obadiah as well; the book bearing his name is a word of judgment against Edom for gloating over the invasion of Jerusalem. Though the date of Obadiah's oracle is unknown, it is almost certainly about the Babylonian invasion that Ezekiel spoke of. Read Obadiah 1:11-14. Write down *all the verbs* that describe what Edom did while Jerusalem was being plundered.

_____

_____

The hearers of Jesus' Sermon on the Mount knew the history of how Israel had been mistreated by many nations over the centuries. How would Jesus' words have clashed with and challenged their natural feelings about their enemies?

CHAMPION JUDGES

The Old Testament "judgmental champions" were Job's "comforters." After Job lost his worldly wealth, his children and his health, three of his friends came to comfort him. For seven days and nights they sat with him and did not say anything (Job 2:11-13). They should have stayed quiet. After Job broke the silence and questioned why these disasters had happened to him, they began to tell him that it was all his fault.

For a sample of their advice, read the words of Eliphaz in Job 22. Check any of the following ideas that you find expressed in the passage:

_____ God is punishing Job for mistreating the poor and helpless.

_____ God has already forgiven Job's sins.

_____ Job deserves what he is getting.

_____ Job can be forgiven if he returns to God.

_____ Job is one of the wisest people in the land.

_____ Job's prosperity will return once he submits to God.

_____ Job is innocent but is suffering anyway.

At the end of the book of Job, God finally speaks, silencing everyone (Job 38–41). Read Job 42:7-9. What did the Lord have to say about whether Job's judgmental friends were right or wrong?

_____

_____

_____

Job's friends were so busy trying to get the speck out of Job's eye that they did not see the planks in their own eyes. What God told Job's friends is essentially the same as Jesus' warning against judging in the Sermon on the Mount. The principle was as true in Job's time as it was in Jesus' time and as it is now.

DEALING WITH PIGHEADED PEOPLE

The ancient Hebrews were closely connected with various domesticated animals such as cattle, sheep, goats, camels and donkeys. However, there is no Old Testament record of domesticated dogs living with people as companions or for work such as hunting or herding. Job 30:1 has an isolated reference to "sheep dogs," but even that has a scornful tone. Old Testament references to dogs are images of contempt, self-abasement or wickedness. As scholar W. Steward McCullough notes, "The dogs of the Bible . . . appear to have been the scavenger sort, which haunted the streets and refuse dumps of the towns and which were generally considered to be unclean and vicious."[1]

To the Israelites, pigs were even more abhorrent than dogs. The pig was one of the unclean animals that Jews were forbidden to eat or even to touch (Leviticus 11:7).

We sometimes refer to inflexible people as "pigheaded." While Scripture does not allow scorning any human being made in the image of God, we are counseled to use wisdom about where and on whom to expend our energies.

How would you sum up the advice of the following Proverbs about trying to deal with stubbornly unreasonable people?

Proverbs 15:12; 17:12; 18:2; 20:3

_____

_____

_____

In your opinion or from your own experience, what is a good way to pray for such people?

_____

_____

_____

_____

ASK, SEEK, KNOCK

In Matthew 7:7-8 when Jesus encouraged his hearers to ask, seek and knock, he invited them to do as many people throughout the Old Testament had done: to pray to God for what they needed, or at least what they thought they needed.

At the time of the Babylonian conquest of Jerusalem, God spoke encouraging words to a defeated people about how he would answer their prayers. Nebuchadnezzar had already deported many Jews to Babylon. The situation looked bleak. Through the prophet Jeremiah, who remained in Jerusalem, God sent the exiles a message of hope and reassurance.

In what spirit and attitude does God tell the people to pray to him?

_____

_____

_____

_____

What does God promise to do in response to their prayers?

_____

_____

_____

_____

THE FATHER PROVIDES

References to *bread* in the Old Testament are too many to enumerate. From earliest times, bread has been the staple of the everyday diet.

At the beginning of Scripture, for example, the word *food* in our English Bible is literally the Hebrew word *bread* in God's curse on Adam after the Fall:[2]

> By the sweat of your brow
>> you will eat your food
> until you return to the ground,
>> since from it you were taken;
> for dust you are
>> and to dust you will return. (Genesis 3:19)

Although Adam had to work for his food, God was ultimately the provider of the food. God has continued to provide for humanity throughout our history, using the processes of nature combined with our work.

The provision of bread comes through sowing, harvest, milling and baking. During the years in the wilderness after they left Egypt, the Israelites experienced a miraculous bypassing of these usual means. In session 8 you read about God's provision of manna. Read more of the account in Exodus 16:13-36.

How does the provision of manna demonstrate God's faithfulness to his people?

_____

_____

_____

_____

How was faith involved in the people's gathering of manna?

_____

_____

_____

_____

Jesus' words about fathers and children (Matthew 7:9-11) presuppose a society in which the father is the provider of good and necessary things to his children.

Read 1 Samuel 17:12-19. How did Jesse demonstrate his concern and his generosity toward his sons, even over a considerable distance?

_____

_____

_____

_____

Jesus' reassuring words about the Father in heaven would have resonated with people who were familiar with both the role of earthly fathers and the history of God's care for Israel. Here Jesus was not introducing something new and revolutionary, but was calling on something which the minds and hearts of all his hearers would recognize.

---

[1]W. Steward McCullough, "Dog," in *Interpreter's Dictionary of the Bible,* ed. George Arthur Buttrick (Nashville: Abingdon Press, 1962), 1:862.

[2]W. E. Vine, *Vines Complete Expository Dictionary of Old and New Testament Words* (Nashville: Thomas Nelson, 1996), p. 24.

A Christian's Relationships

TO OUR BROTHERS AND SISTERS AND TO OUR FATHER

Jesus does not anticipate that the Christian community will be perfect. On the contrary, he assumes both that there will be misdemeanors and that these will give rise to tensions and problems in relationships. In such a situation he forbids two alternatives, then commends a third, better, more Christian way.

Jesus' words "Do not judge, or you too will be judged" are well known but much misunderstood. The context does not refer to judges in courts of law but rather to the responsibility of individuals to one another. It cannot be understood as a command to suspend our critical faculties in relation to other people and to refuse to distinguish between good and evil. We can be sure of this because much of Christ's teaching in the Sermon on the Mount is based on the assumption that we will (indeed should) use our critical powers. The very command not to judge is followed by two further commands: not to give what is sacred to dogs or throw pearls to pigs, and to watch out for false prophets (Matthew 5:6, 15). It would be impossible to obey either of these commands without using our critical judgment.

Then what did Jesus mean by "judging"? In a word, *censoriousness*. The censorious critic is a faultfinder who is negative and destructive toward other people and enjoys actively seeking out their failings. To be censorious is to claim the competence and authority to sit in judgment upon one's fellow human being. To be censorious is to presume arrogantly to anticipate the day of judgment, to usurp the prerogative of the divine Judge, in fact to try to play God. If we dare to judge others, we shall be judged with greater strictness ourselves, because we cannot plead ignorance of the law we claim to be able to administer. To sum up, the command not to judge is not a requirement to be blind, but rather a plea to be generous.

Jesus' famous little parable about foreign bodies in the eye is another reason why we are unfit to be judges: not only because we are fallible human beings but also because we are fallen human beings. We have a fatal tendency to exaggerate the faults of others and minimize the gravity of our own. What we are often doing is seeing our own faults in others and judging them vicariously. That way we experience the pleasure of self-righteousness without the pain of penitence. So "you hypocrite" (v. 5) is a key expression here. What we should do instead is to apply to ourselves at least as strict and critical a standard as we apply to others. We need to be as critical of ourselves as we often are of others, and as generous to others as we always are to ourselves.

If we are not to judge others, finding fault with them in a condemning way, neither are we to ignore their faults and pretend that everybody is the same. Jesus' language about dogs and pigs is startling, but the context provides a healthy balance. Who are these "dogs" and "pigs"? Jesus is indicating not only that they are more animals than humans, but that they are animals with dirty habits as well. The dogs he had in mind were not well-behaved lap dogs but wild pariah dogs which scavenged in the city's rubbish dumps. And pigs were unclean animals to the Jew. But Christians certainly do not have to regard non-Christians in this contemptuous way. So what is this "sacred" thing, and what are the "pearls"? It is helpful to find a link with the pearl of great value in Jesus' parable, which refers to the kingdom of God or salvation, and by extension to the gospel (Matthew 13:44-46). The dogs and pigs with whom we are forbidden to share the gospel pearl are not just unbelievers. They must rather be those who have had ample opportunity to hear and receive the good news, but have decisively—even defiantly—rejected it. To persist beyond a certain point in offering the gospel to such people is to invite its rejection with contempt and even blasphemy. At the same time to give people up is a very serious step to take. This teaching of Jesus is for exceptional situations only; our normal Christian duty is to be patient and persevere with others, as God has patiently persevered with us.

It seems natural that Jesus should move on from our relationship with our fellow human beings to our relationship with our heavenly Father. This passage (Matthew 5:7-11) is not the first instruction on prayer in the Sermon on the Mount, but now Jesus actively encourages us to pray by giving us some very gracious promises.

Jesus seeks to imprint his promises on our mind and memory by the hammer blows of repetition. "Ask . . . seek . . . knock" (v. 7). These may deliberately be in an ascending scale of urgency. All three verbs are present imperatives and indicate the persistence with which we should make our requests known to God. Jesus illustrates his promises by a down-to-earth parable (vv. 9-11). If a child asks for something wholesome to eat (bread or fish), will the child receive instead something unwholesome, either inedible (a stone) or positively harmful (a poisonous snake)? Of course not! The force of the parable lies in a contrast rather than a comparison between God and a human parent. If human parents (although evil) know how to give good gifts to their children, how much more will our heavenly Father (who is not evil but wholly good) give good things to those who ask him? There is no doubt that our prayers are transformed when we remember that the God we are coming to is *Abba, Father* and is infinitely good and kind. If

we belong to Christ, God is our Father, we are his children, and prayer is coming to him with our requests.

Prayer sounds very simple when Jesus teaches about it. Just *ask . . . seek . . . knock . . .* and in each case you will be answered. This is a deceptive simplicity, however. First, prayer presupposes knowledge. Since God gives gifts only if they accord with his will, we have to take pains to discover his will. Second, prayer presupposes faith. It is one thing to know God's will; it is another to humble ourselves before him and express our confidence that he is able to cause his will to be done. Third, prayer presupposes desire. We may know God's will and believe he can perform it, and still not desire it. Thus, before we ask, we must know what to ask for and whether it accords with God's will; we must believe God can grant it; and we must genuinely want to receive. Then the gracious promises of Jesus will come true.

Much has been made by various commentators of the fact that the golden rule (v. 12) is found in a similar—but always negative—form elsewhere. There is really an enormous difference between the negative and rather grudging maxim of Hillel ("Do not do to others what is hateful to you") and the positive initiative contained in the instruction of Jesus ("Do to others what you would have them do to you"). It is a high standard because self-love is a powerful force in our lives. Self-advantage often guides us in our own affairs; now we must also let it guide us in our behavior to others. All we have to do is use our imagination, put ourselves in the other person's shoes and ask, "How would I like to be treated in that situation?" Indeed, it is a principle of such wide application that Jesus could add, "for this sums up the Law and the Prophets." That is, those who direct their conduct toward others according to how they would like others to direct theirs toward them have fulfilled the Law and the Prophets, at least in the matter of neighbor-love.

What's the main idea in this section?

What is one thing you can act on based on this reading?

PART 4. DISCUSS
Putting It All Together

OPEN

Would people say that you have been an encouraging presence in the Christian community? Why or why not?

READ MATTHEW 7:1-12.

The Christian counterculture is not just an individual value system and lifestyle, but a community affair. It involves relationships. And the Christian community is in essence a family, God's family. Probably the two strongest elements in our Christian consciousness are an awareness of God as our Father and an awareness of our fellow Christians as our brothers and sisters through Christ, although at the same time we can never forget our responsibility to those outside the family whom we long to see brought in.

1. Why do we often see others' faults so clearly but not our own faults?

2. How were Job's friends an outstanding example of being judgmental?

3. When might it be wise to draw back from presenting the gospel to someone and let the person go?

4. How does Jesus use bread and fish to make a point about prayer and God's generosity?

5. How is the golden rule (Matthew 7:12) a summing up of the Law and the Prophets?

6. What has been your experience of being judged by others?

7. About what or whom do you tend to be judgmental?

8. What "planks" has the Lord shown you that you have in your own eyes?

9. When have you had an answer to prayer after a long time of asking, seeking and knocking?

10. What do you hesitate to pray for, and why do you hesitate?

11. What are you asking, seeking and knocking for most urgently right now?

Bring your responses to question eleven to the Lord together in prayer.

DETECTING THE LIES OF OUR WORLD

Matthew 7:13-20

WHERE WE'RE GOING

In our consumer-oriented society, people would like the opportunity to combine elements of several religions or even to design one of their own, but Jesus will not allow us this comfortable option. He insists that ultimately there is only one choice.

Part 1. Investigate: Matthew 7:13-20 (On Your Own)

Part 2. Connect: Scripture to Scripture (On Your Own)

Part 3. Reflect: A Christian's Relationships: *To False Prophets* (On Your Own)

Part 4. Discuss: Putting It All Together (With a Group)

A PRAYER TO PRAY

Here's a prayer you can use as you begin this session:

Lord Jesus, you are the Way, the Truth and the Life. You are the only one worth following and the only one we can safely follow. To choose your narrow road is to choose the path to life. But the wide road attracts us. It looks easier, and it seems to lead to bigger and better things. You tell us clearly, however, that the wide road leads only to death. Help us to listen to you, and to refuse to listen to false prophets who want to lure us down that road. Give us discernment and perseverance so that we stay on the true Way to the end. Amen.

PART 1. INVESTIGATE
Matthew 7:13-20

Read Matthew 7:13-20.

1. Why are broad gates and false prophets so appealing to people today?

2. How are the two gates described (vv. 13-14)?

3. In what sense is the gate of Christianity small and the road narrow?

4. In what sense is the world's gate wide and its road broad?

5. Why do you think many people dislike the notion that there is only one true gate?

6. Why is it significant that Jesus' warning about false prophets (vv. 15-20) comes immediately after his discussion of the narrow and wide gates?

7. Jesus says that false prophets "come to you in sheep's clothing" (v. 15). What disguises might they wear today (see vv. 21-23)?

7:13-14. *Jesus' hearers would have been familiar with the image of "two ways"—one leading to life and the other to death; it was common in Judaism. Jesus' emphasis that few are on the right way occurs in 4 Ezra [a book of the Apocrypha] but is not as common as the general image of the two ways. Most Jewish people believed that Israel as a whole would be saved and that the few who were lost would be exceptions to the general rule.*

7:15. *Although most educated Jewish people did not believe that prophets had continued in the Old Testament sense, they believed that false prophets (cf., e.g., Jer 2:8; 5:30) continued; Josephus mentioned many of them in the first century. The contrast between vicious wolves and harmless lambs or sheep was proverbial.*

7:16. *Like wheat and barley, grapes and figs were among the most valuable and widely consumed fruits of the earth; thorns and thistles were worthless and troublesome to harvesters, as the Old Testament often mentions.*

7:17-20. *The repetition of "know them by their fruits" (7:17, 20) brackets this illustration; such bracketing was commonly used as a literary device (called inclusio) to mark off a paragraph. Prophets were known to be false if they led people away from the true God (Deut 13) or their words did not come to pass (Deut 18:21-22). The rabbis allowed that prophets might temporarily suspend a teaching of the law the way rabbis themselves would, but if they denied the law itself or advocated idolatry, they were false prophets. Jesus teaches that if they do not live right, they are false (Mt 7:21-23). Cf. Luke 6:43-45.*

8. What false messages or prophecies have you heard recently? How could you tell they were false?

9. In what sense are these false prophets like ferocious wolves?

10. Jesus also says, "By their fruit you will recognize them" (v. 16). What kind of fruit does he have in mind?

How can the quality of the fruit reveal the quality of the tree?

11. How can we keep from becoming "witch hunters" as we seek to recognize false prophets?

12. "Every tree that does not bear good fruit is cut down and thrown into the fire" (v. 19). How can this warning to false prophets also keep us from becoming complacent as Christians?

Pray that you will know the truth and have the courage to enter through the narrow gate.

PART 2. CONNECT
Scripture to Scripture

THE TWO WAYS

In the Sermon on the Mount, Jesus called for a choice between the narrow gate and road, which lead to life, and the wide gate and road, which lead to destruction. His hearers would have been familiar with the choice offered by God between life and death.

Shortly before Moses died, when the Israelites were about enter Canaan under the leadership of Joshua, Moses presented them with a similar choice, although he did not refer to the narrowness or breadth of the gates and roads.

Read Deuteronomy 30:11-20. What was promised as a result of

        obedience?   disobedience?

What additional motivations were the Israelites given to urge them to "choose life" (vv. 19-20)?

_____

_____

_____

_____

Psalm 1 also offers a sharp contrast between two ways: the way of the righteous person and the way of the wicked person. It finds no in-between state or compromise between the two. Read Psalm 1.

What does the righteous person do?

_____

_____

_____

_____

What does the righteous person *not* do?

_____

_____

_____

_____

What will be the contrasting fates of the two kinds of people?

_____

_____

_____

_____

_____

In your own words, paraphrase Psalm 1:6.

_____

_____

_____

_____

TRUE AND FALSE PROPHETS

When we think of Old Testament prophets, our minds go to the major ones whose prophecies became books of the Bible: Samuel, Isaiah, Jeremiah, Ezekiel, Daniel. We might also think of Moses, Elijah and Elisha, and of the twelve "minor prophets" whose books close out our Old Testament. (They are called *minor* not because they're trivial or less important but because their books are brief.)

There are, however, many other prophets in the Old Testament, those whose time on the stage of the Old Testament is brief but essential. They appear for a scene or two to play some key role at a crisis in Israel's history. Some are named, such as Ahijah, who prophesied that Jeroboam would rule over the ten northern tribes (1 Kings 11:29-39). Others are unnamed, such as the prophet who cried out against Jeroboam's idolatrous altar at Bethel (1 Kings 13:1-6).

It was only reasonable that the Israelites would wonder how they could know whether a supposed prophet had a genuine message from the Lord—so he gave them some guidelines for discernment. They would know a prophet was real, God said, if the events he or she foretold came true (Deuteronomy 18:21-22). The "coming true" test was not 100 percent conclusive, however. There was also the test of loyalty to the Lord as the one true God.

Read Deuteronomy 13:1-5. Respond to the following statements as true or false:

_____ False prophets had to be put to death because they tested the people.

_____ All prophets foretold events, but only the word of genuine prophets came true.

_____ False prophets told people to worship the Lord, but in unacceptable ways.

_____ The people were to test the prophets, but the Lord was also testing the people through false prophets.

_____ False prophets had to be put to death because they could influence the people to rebel against the Lord.

When the Babylonians were threatening Jerusalem, the prophet Jeremiah told the people to submit to the invaders. As a result he was not very popular! The leaders and people preferred to listen to false prophets who said that everything would be fine and Jerusalem would be spared.

Read Jeremiah 23:16-32.

Where did the false prophets get their ideas?

_____

_____

_____

_____

What would have prevented them from speaking falsely?

_____

_____

_____

_____

Read Jeremiah 26:7-12. Here we see a true prophet of God responding to vicious opposition. How did Jeremiah both defend his integrity and express his trust in the Lord?

_____

_____

_____

_____

SHEEP AND WOLVES

Jesus said that false prophets "come to you in sheep's clothing, but inwardly they are ferocious wolves" (Matthew 7:15).

The economy of Israel depended on sheep, cattle and goats, which grazed in flocks and herds in open country. In such a vulnerable setting, predators were a constant threat. The wolf was feared most. In Scripture the wolf "emerges from a dozen references as an animal of particular ferocity." Details of wolves' fierceness in Scripture "present a heightened picture of terror and ferocity, which provides the context for the revulsion that biblical writers and Jesus have toward evil people and institutions that they compare to wolves."[1]

From what you have just read in Deuteronomy 13 and Jeremiah 23 and 26, how is the comparison between a false prophet and a wolf masquerading as a sheep an accurate comparison?

GOOD AND BAD FRUIT

Grapes and figs were important to the diet and the economy of Israel. A keeper of vineyards or fig trees hoped for high-quality fruit. What a disappointment—perhaps even an economic disaster—if there was only fruit of poor quality.

When the Israelites came to the border of Canaan, Moses sent twelve men to spy out the land they were about to enter. Moses wanted to ascertain both the strength of the people and the fertility of the soil.

The spies gathered more than intelligence. Read Numbers 13:17-25. What evidence did the spies bring back that Canaan was a productive land?

_____

_____

_____

_____

_____

Write a brief imaginary dialogue between the two carriers of the pole (v. 23) as they head back toward the Israelite camp.

_____

_____

_____

_____

_____

Now how might the Israelites have responded when they saw the spies return with their evidence of the land's fruitfulness?

_____

_____

_____

_____

_____

In the Sermon on the Mount, Jesus urged his followers to discern between bad fruit and good fruit. We are not left in the dark about the reliability of prophets and teachers; their fruit reveals the motives of their hearts. The Israelite spies' gladness in finding the fruit of Canaan was a foretaste of Christians' gladness when we recognize the good fruit of godly prophets and teachers.

---

[1]Leland Ryken, James C. Wilhoit and Tremper Longman III, eds., "Wolf," *Dictionary of Biblical Imagery* (Downers Grove, IL: InterVarsity Press, 1998), p. 958.

Matthew 7:13-14 is striking for the absolute nature of the choice before us. We would all prefer to be given many more choices than only one, or better still to fuse them all into a conglomerate religion. Jesus insists that ultimately there is only one choice because there are only two possibilities to choose from.

First, there are *two roads*. One road is broad. There is plenty of room on it for diversity of opinions and laxity of morals. It is the road of tolerance and permissiveness. Travelers on this road follow their own inclinations, that is, the desires of the human heart in its fallenness. No effort is required to learn superficiality, self-love, hypocrisy, mechanical religion, false ambition or censoriousness. That is why the broad road is easy.

The hard road, on the other hand, is narrow. Its boundaries are clearly marked. Its narrowness is due to something called *divine revelation*, which restricts pilgrims to the confines of what God has revealed in Scripture to be true and good. Revealed truth imposes a limitation on what Christians may believe, and revealed goodness on how we may behave. In a sense this is hard. Yet Christ's hard and narrow way is also to be welcomed as his "easy yoke" and "light burden" (Matthew 11:30).

Secondly, there are *two gates*. The gate leading to the easy way is wide, for it is a simple matter to get onto the easy road. We need leave nothing behind, not even our sins, self-righteousness or pride. The gate leading to the hard way, on the other hand, is narrow. One has to look for it to find it. Further, in order to enter it we must leave everything behind—sin, selfish ambition, covetousness, even if necessary family and friends. For no one can follow Christ who has not fully denied himself or

herself. How can we find this gate? It is Jesus Christ himself. "I am the gate; whoever enters through me will be saved" (John 10:9).

Thirdly, there are *two destinations*. Jesus taught that the easy way, entered by the wide gate, leads to destruction. He did not define what he meant by this, and presumably the precise nature of hell is as much beyond our finite understanding as the precise nature of heaven. But the terrible word *destruction* seems to give us liberty to say that everything good will be destroyed in hell—love and loveliness, beauty and truth, joy, peace and hope—and that forever. It is a prospect too awful to contemplate without tears. For the broad road is the suicide road.

By contrast, the hard way, entered by the narrow gate, leads to *life,* even to that eternal life which Jesus explained in terms of fellowship with God, beginning here but perfected hereafter, in which we see and share his glory and find perfect fulfillment as human beings in the selfless service of him and of our fellows.

Fourthly, there are *two crowds*. Entering by the wide gate and traveling along the easy road to destruction are *many*. It is a busy freeway. The narrow and hard road which leads to life seems to be comparatively deserted. *Only a few find it.* Jesus seems to have anticipated that his followers would be (or at least would appear to be and feel themselves to be) a despised minority movement. I do not think we can build on this contrast between *few* and *many* any speculation that the final number of God's redeemed will be small. If we compare Scripture with Scripture, we shall put alongside this teaching of Jesus the vision of John that the redeemed before God's throne will be "a great multitude that no one could count"

(Revelation 7:9). When someone asked Jesus if only a few people were going to be saved, he declined to satisfy their curiosity. Instead he replied, "Make every effort to enter through the narrow door" (Luke 13:24).

To recapitulate, there are according to Jesus only two ways, easy and hard (there is no middle way), entered by two gates, broad and narrow (there is no other gate), trodden by two crowds, large and small (there is no neutral group), ending in two destinations, destruction and life (there is no third alternative).

Jesus then speaks of the perils of false teachers. In telling people to "watch out for false prophets," Jesus obviously assumed that they already exist. We come across them in the Old Testament, and Jesus seems to have regarded the Pharisees and the Sadducees in the same light. He also implied that they would increase, and that the period preceding the end would be characterized not only by the worldwide spread of the gospel but also by the rise of false teachers who would lead many astray (Matthew 24:11-14).

In telling us to beware of false prophets Jesus made another assumption, that there is an objective standard of truth from which the falsehood of the false prophets is to be distinguished. The very notion of "false" prophets is meaningless otherwise. Jesus was no syncretist, teaching that contradictory opinions were in reality complementary insights into the same truth. He held that truth and falsehood excluded one another, and that those who propagate lies in God's name are false prophets, of whom his followers must be aware.

From Jesus' metaphor of sheep and wolves we learn that pseudoprophets are both dangerous and deceptive. Their danger is that in reality they are wolves. A good shepherd, Jesus was to teach later, was always on the lookout for wolves in order to protect the sheep, whereas the hired laborer would abandon them at the sight of a wolf, leaving it to attack and scatter the flock (John 10:11-13). Just so,

Christ's flock is at the mercy of either good shepherds, paid laborers or wolves. The good pastor feeds the flock with truth, the false teacher divides it by error, while the time-serving professional does nothing to protect it but abandons it to false teachers.

It is no accident that Jesus' warning about false prophets immediately follows his teaching about the two ways. False prophets are adept at blurring the issue of salvation. Some so muddle or distort the gospel that they make it hard for seekers to find the narrow gate. Others try to make out that the narrow way is in reality much broader than Jesus implied, and that to walk it requires little if any restriction on one's belief or behavior. Yet others, perhaps the most pernicious of all, dare to contradict Jesus and to assert that the broad road does not lead to destruction, but that all roads lead to God. These false teachers, whom Jesus likened to ferocious wolves, are responsible for leading some people to the very destruction which they say does not exist.

The false prophets are more than dangerous; they are also deceptive. The dogs and pigs of verse 6, because of their dirty habits, are easy to recognize. But not the wolves, for they sneak into the flock in the disguise of sheep. As a result, the unwary actually mistake them for sheep and give them an unsuspecting welcome. Their true character is not discovered until the damage has been done. "Watch out!" Jesus warns. The false teacher claims to be a teacher of the truth. We must look beneath the appearance to the reality. What lives under the fleece: a sheep or a wolf?

We are now ready to look at the tests Jesus told us to apply to prophets. Here he changed his metaphor from sheep and wolves to trees and their fruit. In doing so he moved from the risk of nonrecognition to the means of recognition. No tree can hide its identity for long. Noxious weeds like thorns and thistles simply cannot produce edible fruit like grapes and figs. The conclusion which Jesus emphasized twice is that "by their fruit you will recognize them."

The first kind of fruit by which false prophets reveal their true identity is in the realm of character and conduct. Whenever we see in a teacher the meekness and gentleness of Christ, his love, patience, kindness, goodness and self-control, we have reason to believe that teacher to be true, not false. On the other hand, whenever these qualities are missing, and the works of the flesh are more apparent than the fruit of the Spirit, we are justified in suspecting that the prophet is an impostor.

But a prophet's "fruits" are not only character and manner of life. A second fruit is the person's actual teaching. If a person's heart is revealed in the person's words, as a tree is known by its fruit, we have a responsibility to test a teacher by his or her teaching. The apostle John gives us an example of this. To moral tests he added a doctrinal one. In general this was whether the teacher's message was in accord with the original apostolic instruction, and in particular whether it confessed Jesus as the Christ come in the flesh, thus acknowledging his divine-human person (1 John 2:22-24; 4:2-3; 2 John 7-9).

Then I think there is a third test which we must apply to teachers, and this concerns their influence. We have to ask ourselves what effect their teaching has on their followers. Sometimes the falsity of false teaching is not immediately apparent, but becomes apparent only in its disastrous results. It upsets people's faith, promotes ungodliness and causes bitter divisions. Sound teaching, by contrast, produces faith, love and godliness.

Fruit takes time to grow. We have to wait for it patiently. We also need an opportunity to examine it closely, for it is not always possible to recognize a tree and its fruit from a distance. To apply this to a teacher, what is needed is not a superficial estimate of the person's standing in the church, but a close and critical scrutiny of his or her character, conduct, message, motives and influence.

What's the main idea in this section?

What is one thing you can act on based on this reading?

PART 4. DISCUSS
Putting It All Together

OPEN

If God hired a consultant to help him improve his image among twenty-first-century North Americans, what character qualities would the consultant want to emphasize? What changes might the consultant suggest God make in order to become more popular?

READ MATTHEW 7:13-20.

In the Sermon on the Mount the contrast between the two kinds of righteousness and devotion, the two treasures, the two masters and the two ambitions has been faithfully portrayed; now the time for decision has come. Is it to be the kingdom of Satan or the kingdom of God, the prevailing culture or the Christian counter-culture?

1. Why does Jesus describe the gate that leads to him as small, and the road narrow?

2. Why is the broader road more attractive to so many people?

3. Think of examples of false prophets you know about (that is, pseudo-Christian cults which use the right language but teach aberrant doctrine). What is their appeal?

4. Why are false prophets so dangerous (remember to speak with grace and sensitivity)?

5. What does good fruit look like?

6. How have you found what Jesus said about his way in vv. 13-14 to be true?

7. What would you say to a person who has been on the wide road but is feeling dissatisfied?

8. If you were once on the wide road yourself, what turned you around?

9. Have you ever been taken in by a false teacher or seen someone close to you taken in by a false teacher? With what results?

10. Have you ever discerned a false teacher? How did you tell the difference?

11. What will you do this week to become more aware of your choices between the broad and narrow ways?

Pray that you will grow in your discernment, without going to the extreme of being suspicious of everything and everyone. Pray that you will also bear good fruit in your character, doctrine and influence.

MAKING THE CHOICE
OF A LIFETIME

Matthew 7:21-29

WHERE WE'RE GOING

The two final paragraphs of the Sermon are very similar. Both contrast the wrong and the right responses to Christ's teaching. Both show that neutrality is impossible and that a definite decision has to be made. Both stress that nothing can take the place of an active, practical obedience. And both teach that the issue of life and death on the day of judgment will be determined by our moral response to Christ and his teaching in this life. The only difference between the paragraphs is that in the first people offer a profession of their lips as an alternative to obedience, and in the second they offer a hearing with their ears.

    Part 1. Investigate: Matthew 7:21-29 (On Your Own)

    Part 2. Connect: Scripture of Scripture (On Your Own)

    Part 3. Reflect: A Christian's Commitment: *The Radical Choice* (On Your Own)

    Part 4. Discuss: Putting It All Together (With a Group)

A PRAYER TO PRAY

Here's a prayer you can use to begin this final session of your study:

Lord Jesus, you are the Lord of the universe, and we say you are the Lord of our lives. Yet we know how easy it is to say "Lord, Lord" and then go our own way and not obey you. Make us people who live what we say. Melt our stubborn hearts and humble our pride so that we submit to you as Lord in every way and obey you wholeheartedly. We pray this in the name of Jesus, who is our strong foundation. Amen.

PART 1. INVESTIGATE
Matthew 7:21-29

Read Matthew 7:21-29.

1. Describe the various types of people Jesus talks about in these verses. How does each respond to Jesus' teaching?

2. On the surface, what might we admire about those described in verses 21-23?

7:24. *The rabbis debated whether hearing or doing the law was more important; most concluded that hearing it was more important, because one could not do it without hearing it. But they did insist that both were necessary.*

3. In spite of their admirable statements or actions, why does Jesus condemn such people?

4. Why do people so often confuse religious activity with doing the will of the Father?

How do you understand the difference?

7:24-27. *Again the image is of the day of judgment. The idea of ultimately being judged for hearing but not obeying was familiar (Ezek 33:32-33). But no Jewish teacher apart from Jesus claimed so much authority for his own words; such authority was reserved for the law itself. Some of Jesus' more biblically literate hearers may have thought of Proverbs 24:3 ("by wisdom a house is built") and the contrast between wisdom (which builds a house in 9:1) and folly in Proverbs 9:1-18.*

5. How were the two houses similar and different (vv. 24-27)?

6. Why is it often difficult to tell the difference between genuine Christians and counterfeit ones?

7. How did the storms reveal what was previously unseen?

8. What kinds of storms have you faced in life? What did they reveal about the quality of your life?

9. The crowds were amazed at Jesus' teaching, because he taught as one who had authority (vv. 28-29). In what ways was Jesus' authority demonstrated in his Sermon?

7:28-29. *The teachers of the law never claimed as much authority as Jesus had (7:24-27); they derived their authority especially from building on previous tradition.*

10. What difference does it make to you that Jesus taught with authority (v. 29)?

11. How do verses 21-29 provide a fitting conclusion to the Sermon on the Mount?

12. What are some of the "words" of Jesus you have heard in the Sermon on the Mount (v. 24) that you want to have stick with you?

Ask the Lord to help you submit to his authority, especially in those areas where you feel disobedient or hypocritical.

PART 2. CONNECT
Scripture to Scripture

EMPTY ADORATION

It was not only in New Testament times that people said "Lord, Lord" and failed to match their words with deeds. Several of the prophets carried a message from the Lord warning people about merely paying him lip service. Take, for example, these words from Isaiah:

> The Lord says:
> "These people come near to me with their mouth
> and honor me with their lips,
> but their hearts are far from me.
> Their worship of me
> is based on merely human rules they have been taught." (Isaiah 29:13)

The prophet Ezekiel received a similar message from the Lord. He was exiled to Babylon several years before the actual conquest and destruction of the city of Jerusalem. The Lord led Ezekiel to prophesy in some outlandish ways, but the exiles were apparently favorably disposed toward him and willing to come and at least listen. That's where their willingness stopped, however.

Read Ezekiel 33:30-33. This is part of "the word of the Lord" which came to Ezekiel after he received word that Jerusalem had fallen to the Babylonians.

Why do you think the people went to hear Ezekiel?

_____

_____

_____

_____

What evidence did they give that they did not really believe his message?

_____

_____

_____

_____

EMPTY PROPHECY

Jesus spoke of those who would protest that in the name of the Lord they had prophesied, driven out demons and even performed miracles (Matthew 7:22). In Ezekiel's time there were those among the exiles who made the same claims. This was still before the final destruction of Jerusalem, and they were optimistically prophesying that the city would not fall.

Read Ezekiel 13:1-16.

What was the message of the false prophets?

_____

_____

_____

_____

What was the Lord's message?

_____

_____

_____

_____

What adjectives did the Lord use to describe the false prophets?

_____

_____

_____

_____

What adjectives did the Lord use to describe the false prophets' divinations (prophecies)?

_____

_____

_____

_____

The Lord compares the false prophecies to a flimsy wall covered with whitewash (v. 10). What forces will come against that wall (vv. 11, 13)?

_____

_____

_____

_____

Sketch the scene of what happens to the flimsy whitewashed wall of false prophecies—and to the prophets themselves (vv. 11-14).

The *Dictionary of Biblical Imagery* sheds further light on the illustration: "Biblical buildings and cities were only as substantial as their foundations, which were symbolically related to the behavior of the people. Thus houses and walls might be impressively painted, yet without deep foundations they were flimsy and insecure. In catastrophic judgments the 'exposure of foundations' meant complete destruction (Deut 32:22; Ps 18:15; Ezek 13:14; Lk 6:49)."[1]

The Old Testament witness is consistent: ungodliness leads to insecurity, weakness and eventual collapse. Godliness, on the other hand, will last to eternity.

WISDOM AND FOLLY

The Old Testament has much to say about wisdom and folly. The difference between the wise person and the fool has nothing to do with education or inborn intelligence. It has everything to do with whether the person acknowledges, reveres and obeys the Lord: "The fool says in his heart, 'There is no God'" (Psalm 14:1) while on the other hand "The fear of the LORD is the beginning of wisdom; all who follow his precepts have good understanding" (Psalm 111:10).

The book of Proverbs draws absolute contrasts between the wise person and the fool. Chapter 9 of Proverbs personifies Wisdom and Folly as two women who call out to people passing by, inviting them to come in and partake of what each has to offer.

Read Proverbs 9:1-18.

As a general statement, what does Wisdom offer?

_____

_____

_____

_____

As a general statement, what does Folly offer?

_____

_____

_____

_____

What do the following proverbs say about the wise person and the fool?

	Wise Person	**Fool**
Proverbs 1:7		
Proverbs 10:14		
Proverbs 12:15		
Proverbs 14:1		
Proverbs 14:3		
Proverbs 14:16		
Proverbs 28:26		
Proverbs 29:11		

Fill in the missing parts of Proverbs 24:3-4:

"By _____,

    and through _____ it is established;

through _____ its rooms are filled

    with _____."

---

[1]Leland Ryken, James C. Wilhoit and Tremper Longman, eds., "Foundation," in *Dictionary of Biblical Imagery* (Downers Grove, IL: InterVarsity Press, 1998), p. 306.

PART 3. REFLECT
A Christian's Commitment
THE RADICAL CHOICE

At this point in the Sermon on the Mount, Jesus is not concerned to add further instruction, but rather to ensure a proper response to the instruction he has already given. So Jesus confronts us with himself, sets before us the radical choice between obedience and disobedience, and calls us to an unconditional commitment of mind, will and life to his teaching. He warns us of two unacceptable alternatives, first a merely verbal profession (Matthew 7:21-23) and secondly a merely intellectual knowledge (vv. 24-27).

In verses 21-23 the people Jesus describes are relying for salvation on a creedal affirmation, on what they "say" to or about Christ. But our final destiny will be settled, Jesus insists, neither by what we are saying to him today, nor by what we shall say to him on the last day, but by whether we do what we say, whether our verbal profession is accompanied by moral obedience.

Now a verbal profession of Christ is indispensable. In order to be saved, wrote Paul, we have to confess with our lips and believe in our hearts (Romans 10:9-10). And a true profession of Jesus as Lord is impossible without the Holy Spirit (1 Corinthians 12:3). Moreover, the kind of Christian profession Jesus describes appears to be wholly admirable. Here are people who call Jesus "Lord" with courtesy, orthodoxy and enthusiasm, in private devotion and in public ministry. What can be wrong with this? Everything is wrong because it is talk without truth, profession without reality. It will not save them on the day of judgment.

So Jesus moves on from what *they* are saying and will say to him to what *he* will say to them. He too will make a solemn profession.

The word used in verse 23 is *homologēsō,* "I will confess." Christ's confession to them will be like theirs in being public, but unlike theirs in being true. He will address to them the terrible words "I never knew you. Away from me, you evildoers!"

The reason for their rejection by him is that their profession was verbal, not moral. It concerned their lips only, and not their life. They called Jesus "Lord, Lord" but never submitted to his lordship or obeyed the will of his heavenly Father. Luke's version of this saying is stronger still: "Why do you call me, 'Lord, Lord,' and do not do what I say?" (Luke 6:46).

We who claim to be Christians in our day have made a profession of faith in Jesus privately in conversion and publicly in baptism and/or confirmation. But he is not impressed by our pious and orthodox words. He still asks for evidence of our sincerity in good works of obedience.

Jesus then offers a slightly different contrast. The contrast in Matthew 7:21-23 is between *saying* and doing; the contrast in verses 24-27 is between *hearing* and doing. Jesus illustrates the contrast between his obedient and disobedient hearers by his well-known parable of the two builders, the wise person who "dug down deep" (Luke 6:48) and constructed his house on rock, and the fool who could not be bothered with foundations and was content to build on sand. As both got on with their building, a casual observer would not have noticed any difference between them. For the difference was in the foundations, and foundations are not seen.

In the same way professing Christians, both the genuine and spurious, often look alike. Both are members of the visible Christian community. Both appear to be building Christian lives. The reason you often cannot tell the difference between them is that the deep foundations of their lives are hidden from view. The real question is not whether they *hear* Christ's teaching, nor even whether they respect or believe it, but whether they *do* what they hear. Only a storm will reveal the truth.

In these final two paragraphs Jesus is insisting that the question is not whether we *say* nice, polite, orthodox, enthusiastic things to or about Jesus, nor whether we *hear* his words (listening, studying, pondering and memorizing them), but whether we *do* what we say and *do* what we know, in other words whether the lordship of Jesus which we profess is one of our life's major realities.

This is not to teach that the way of salvation is by good works of obedience, for the whole New Testament offers salvation only by the sheer grace of God through faith. What Jesus is stressing is that those who truly hear the gospel and profess faith will always obey him, expressing their faith in their works.

In applying this teaching to ourselves, we need to consider that the Bible is a dangerous book to read, and that the church is a dangerous society to join. For in reading the Bible we hear the words of Christ, and in joining the church we say we believe in Christ. As a result, we belong to the company described by Jesus as both hearing his teaching and calling him Lord. Our membership therefore lays upon us the serious responsibility of ensuring that what we know and what we say is translated into what we do.

Thus the Sermon on the Mount ends on the same note of radical choice of which we have been aware throughout. Jesus does not set before his followers a string of easy ethical rules, so much as a set of values and ideals which is entirely distinctive from the way of the world. He summons us to renounce the prevailing secular culture in favor of the Christian counterculture. Instead of conforming to this world—whether in the form of religious Pharisees or of irreligious pagans—we are called by Jesus to imitate our heavenly Father.

The overriding purpose of the Sermon on the Mount is to present us with this alternative, and so to face us with the indispensable necessity of choice. This is why the Sermon's conclusion is so appropriate, as Jesus sketches the two ways (narrow and broad) and the two buildings (on rock and sand). It would be impossible to exaggerate the importance of the choice between them, since once way leads to life while the other ends in destruction, and one building is secure while the other is overwhelmed with disaster. Far more momentous than the choice even of a life work or of a life partner is the choice about life itself. Which road are we going to travel? On which foundation are we going to build?

What's the main idea in this section?

What is one thing you can act on based on this reading?

PART 4. DISCUSS
Putting It All Together

OPEN

What reasons might others have to consider you a wise person? What reasons might others have to consider you a fool?

READ MATTHEW 7:21-29.

The most momentous decision a person will ever make—more than the choice of a career or life partner—is the choice about life itself. How will I react to Jesus?

1. The reflection says, "We need to consider that the Bible is a dangerous book to read, and that the church is a dangerous society to join." Do you agree or disagree, and why?

2. What are some practical examples of people saying "Lord, Lord" while not doing the will of the Father?

3. In verses 24-27 how are the two "houses" similar, and how are they different?

4. What are some "sand" foundations on which people try to build their lives?

5. From "Connect: Scripture to Scripture," what are some of the characteristics of a wise person? of a fool?

6. When you read verses 21-23, do you feel nervous or reassured, and why?

7. When has a showy but false religion seemed attractive to you or to someone you know, and why?

8. Who do you know that has built a spiritual house on rock and withstood storms?

9. What is a storm you have experienced that revealed whether your spiritual house was built on sand or rock?

10. What difference does the authority of Jesus make in your life?

11. Think of one teaching from the Sermon that has challenged you most. How can you begin putting it into practice?

Pray that you will be wise and that you will always build wisely on the foundation of Christ.

GUIDELINES FOR LEADERS

My grace is sufficient for you.

2 CORINTHIANS 12:9

*I*f leading a small group is something new for you, don't worry. You don't need to be an expert on the Bible or a trained teacher. The discussion guides in part four are designed to facilitate a group's discussion, not a leader's presentation. Guiding group members to discover together what the Bible has to say and to listen together for God's guidance will help them remember much more than a lecture would. Furthermore, the discussion guides are designed to flow naturally. You may even find that the discussions seem to lead themselves! They're also flexible; you can use the discussion guide with a variety of groups—students, professionals, coworkers, friends, neighborhood or church groups. Each discussion takes forty-five to sixty minutes in a group setting.

There are some important facts to know about group dynamics and helpful discussion. The suggestions listed below should equip you to effectively and enjoyably fulfill your role as leader.

PREPARING FOR THE STUDY

1. Ask God to help you understand and apply the passage in your own life. Unless this happens, you will not be prepared to lead others. Pray too for the various members of the group. Ask God to open your hearts to the message of his Word and motivate you to action.

2. Carefully work through parts one, two and three of each session before your group meets. Spend time in meditation and reflection as you consider how to respond.

3. Write your thoughts and responses in the space provided in the study guide. This will help you to express your understanding of the passage clearly and more easily remember significant ideas you want to highlight in the group discussion.

4. It may help to have a Bible dictionary handy. Use it to look up any unfamiliar words, names or places.

5. Reflect seriously on how you need to apply the Scripture to your life. Remember that the group members will follow your lead in responding to the studies. They will not go any deeper than you do.

LEADING THE STUDY

1. At the beginning of your first time together, explain that these studies are meant to be discussions, not lectures. Encourage the members of the group to participate. However, do not put pressure on those who may be hesitant to speak—especially during the first few sessions.

2. Be sure that everyone in your group has a study guide. Encourage the group to prepare beforehand for each discussion by reading the introduction to the guide and by working through the questions in each study.

3. Begin each study on time. Open with prayer, asking God to help the group understand and apply the passage.

4. Discuss the "Open" question before the Bible passage is read. It introduces the

theme of the study and helps group members begin to open up. It can also reveal where our thoughts and feelings need to be transformed by Scripture. Encourage as many members as possible to respond to the "Open" question, and be ready to get the discussion going with your own response.

5. Have a group member read aloud the passage to be studied as indicated in the guide.

6. The study questions are designed to be read aloud just as they are written. You may, however, prefer to express them in your own words.

   Note also that there may be times when it is appropriate to deviate from the discussion guide. For example, a question may have already been answered. If so, move on to the next question. Or someone may raise an important question not covered in the guide. Take time to discuss it, but try to keep the group from going off on tangents.

7. Avoid answering your own questions. An eager group quickly becomes passive and silent if members think the leader will do most of the talking. If necessary, repeat or rephrase the question until it is clearly understood, or refer to the commentary woven into the guide to clarify the context or meaning.

8. Don't be afraid of silence in response to the discussion questions. People may need time to think about the question before formulating their answers.

9. Don't be content with just one answer. Ask, "What do the rest of you think?" or "Anything else?" until several people have given answers to the question.

10. Try to be affirming whenever possible. Especially affirm participation. Never reject an answer; if it is clearly off-base, ask, "Which verse led you to that conclusion?" or again, "What do the rest of you think?"

11. Don't expect every answer to be addressed to you, even though this will probably happen at first. As group members become more at ease, they will begin to truly interact with each other. This is one sign of healthy discussion.

12. Don't be afraid of controversy. It can be very stimulating. If you don't resolve an issue completely, don't be frustrated. Explain that the group will move on and God may enlighten all of you in later sessions.

13. Periodically summarize what the group has said about the passage. This helps to draw together the various ideas mentioned and gives continuity to the study. But don't preach.

14. Conclude your time together with the prayer suggestion at the end of the study, adapting it to your group's particular needs as appropriate. Ask for God's help in following through on the applications you've identified.

15. End on time.

Many more suggestions and helps for studying a passage or guiding discussion can be found in *How to Lead a LifeGuide Bible Study* and *The Big Book on Small Groups* (both from InterVarsity Press/USA).

Bibliography

Alexander, T. Desmond, and David W. Baker, eds. *Dictionary of the Old Testament: Pentateuch.* Downers Grove, IL: InterVarsity Press, 2003.

Beale, G. K., and D. A. Carson, eds. *Commentary on the New Testament Use of the Old Testament.* Grand Rapids: Baker Academic, 2007.

Buttrick, George Arthur, ed. *Interpreter's Dictionary of the Bible.* Nashville: Abingdon Press, 1962.

Green, Joel B., Scot McKnight and I. Howard Marshall, eds. *Dictionary of Jesus and the Gospels.* Downers Grove, IL: InterVarsity Press, 1992.

Kaiser, Walter, Jr., Peter H. Davids, F. F. Bruce and Manfred Brauch. *Hard Sayings of the Bible.* Downers Grove, IL: InterVarsity Press, 1996.

Marshall, I. Howard, A. R. Millard, J. I. Packer and D. J. Wiseman, eds. *New Bible Dictionary.* 3rd ed. Downers Grove, IL: InterVarsity Press, 1996.

Ryken, Leland, James C. Wilhoit and Tremper Longman, eds. *Dictionary of Biblical Imagery.* Downers Grove, IL: InterVarsity Press, 1998.

Walton, John H., Victor H. Matthews and Mark W. Chavalas. *The IVP Bible Background Commentary: Old Testament.* Downers Grove, IL: InterVarsity Press, 2000.

Wenham, G. J., J. A. Motyer, D. A. Carson and R. T. France, eds. *New Bible Commentary.* 21st century ed. Downers Grove, IL: InterVarsity Press, 1994.